"Our common practice of prayer is inescapably elusive, open-ended, and somewhat hidden in our faith. In this winsome exposition of prayer, David Williams offers us practical guidance with prayer that is honest, accessible, and filled with insight. Williams walks us through the Lord's Prayer phrase by phrase, with an awareness wrought of real personal engagement and with an eye on contemporary connections. Williams suggests that we can, in our practice, be engaged in 'praying without ceasing.' Those engaged in growth in faith will be grateful for the wise, knowing instruction on offer here."

—**Walter Brueggemann**, biblical scholar and
author of more than one hundred books

"What this profound book offers its reader is the gift of encountering a familiar prayer as if for the first time. Excavating the depths of transformative grace in Jesus's ancient words, *The Prayer of Unwanting* is a timeless and necessary book."

—**Amanda Held Opelt**, songwriter and author of
A Hole in the World and *Holy Unhappiness*

"What do we want when we come to prayer? In *The Prayer of Unwanting*, David Williams looks at Jesus's ancient teachings and winsomely places them into the realities of our own days and desires. If you've ever wondered what prayer is or is meant to be, let these down-to-earth reflections wash over your mind and heart, pointing the way back to Jesus."

—**Catherine McNeil**, author of *Fearing Bravely: Risking Love for Our Neighbors, Strangers, and Enemies*

"Understanding fully how prayer is frequently one of the most unnatural things for us as humans to do, Jesus teaches his disciples how to pray. And in this refreshingly candid, wonderfully childlike exploration of the Lord's Prayer, David Williams invites readers to become more truly themselves by praying it in fresh ways—not to get what we believe we want through praying it, but to get something better than that: the life that is truly life, which we find in Jesus himself."

—**W. David O. Taylor**, associate professor of theology and culture, Fuller Theological Seminary, and author of *Prayers for the Pilgrimage*

The Prayer of Unwanting

THE PRAYER OF
UN
WANTING

HOW THE LORD'S PRAYER HELPS US
GET OVER OURSELVES —
AND WHY THAT MIGHT BE A GOOD THING

DAVID WILLIAMS

BROADLEAF BOOKS
MINNEAPOLIS

THE PRAYER OF UNWANTING
How the Lord's Prayer Helps Us Get Over Ourselves—and Why That
Might Be a Good Thing

29 28 27 26 25 24   1 2 3 4 5 6 7 8 9

Unless otherwise noted, Scripture quotations are taken from the Holy
Bible, New International Version, NIV. Copyright © 1973, 1978, 1984,
2011 by Biblica, Inc.™ Used by permission of Zondervan. All rights
reserved worldwide. www.zondervan.com The "NIV" and "New
International Version" are trademarks registered in the United States
Patent and Trademark Office by Biblica, Inc.™

Library of Congress Cataloging-in-Publication Data

Names: Williams, David, author.
Title: The prayer of unwanting : how the Lord's prayer helps us get over
   ourselves-and why that might be a good thing / David Williams.
Description: Minneapolis : Broadleaf Books, [2025]
Identifiers: LCCN 2024015367 | ISBN 9798889833291 (print) | ISBN
   9798889833307 (ebook)
Subjects: LCSH: Lord's prayer.
Classification: LCC BV230 .W495 2025 | DDC 242/.722—dc23/
   eng/20240807
LC record available at https://lccn.loc.gov/2024015367

Cover design: Juicebox Designs

Print ISBN: 979-8-8898-3329-1
eBook ISBN: 979-8-8898-3330-7

To Deb Platt, for rekindling the light of prayer in my soul

Contents

1. Why We Pray—or Don't   1
2. How Close the Connection   15
3. That Place beyond Place   23
4. Words We Don't Use, Things We Don't Do   31
5. Will You Will   41
6. Necessary Stuff   49
7. The Balance Sheet   59
8. Your Heart's Desire   67
9. The Place of Evil   75
10. The Power and the Glory   85
11. A Mighty Long Time   93
12. Let It Be So   103

Discussion and Reflection Questions   *113*
How and When to Pray the Lord's Prayer   *125*
Acknowledgments   *135*

CHAPTER ONE

Why We Pray—or Don't

I'm not particularly great at praying. Even after fifty-plus years of doing my best to follow Jesus, I often feel fumbly at it, uncertain.

Pastors are supposed to be magically amazing at praying, radiant with our capacity for mystic incantations that summon angels, who are at our beck and call. We're supposed to be sublimely confident, so pray-ey that we'll pray at the drop of a hat.

Not me. Thinking and writing and preaching and discussing? Sure. Stillness and walking meditations? Those I can do. If you call tasks like singing and washing dishes and taking out the trash, in and of themselves, *prayer*, then I'm good.

It's not that the words don't come for me. After twenty years of ministry, words come easy. I can pop off an impromptu prayer at the drop of a hat. My struggle is with the words themselves, with the limitations of human language.

My spoken prayers often feel so small, so inadequate. Here I am, a tiny, ephemeral lump of life, humming the air around me with vibrations that serve as symbolic referents for those who live in my culture. These . . . *sounds* are supposed to impress or convince or change the mind of the Creator of the Universe? They have no more power than the chittering of a frightened squirrel or the angry cawing of crows as they drive away an intruding red-tailed hawk. This is the sort of overthinking we Presbyterians are good at.

Perhaps that's not the struggle you have with prayer. Maybe you're just looking for a way to pray that has meaning. Perhaps you're in a place of challenge where you're so shattered and broken that the right words never fall to hand. I've been in all those places myself.

Or maybe you're yearning to step back into faith after a time away, but the whole idea of prayer still seems awkward or unnatural or pointless. When I returned to the Christian faith in my midtwenties after walking away from it in my late teens, I struggled to pray. Prayer came hard to a pathological overthinker like me. My words always felt inadequate, no more meaningful than chicken scratches in barnyard soil, relative to the Creator of the Universe. No amount of my rambling on meant anything.

But here's the thing: I have learned to pray. I pray—with words—every single day, many times a day. Prayer is how I begin my mornings while I'm lying there and the snooze timer's counting down my minutes. I pray while walking, while running errands, while puttering about the house. I pray a whole bunch when I'm driving on the Beltway or tip-toeing my motorcycle over patches of ice on winding country roads during the winter.

The question is: How? How can average or even deficient pray-ers like me pray? How can we go about this thing called prayer?

***

There are many ways to pray, almost as many as there are human beings. There are also countless books on the subject, some of which I perused as I prepared to write this one.

Being a library sort of person, that's where I went, and there I discovered several shelves of books about prayer: books from mystics, books from pastors, pastel-covered hardback books from tee vee preachers eager to sell you a prayer that'll make you prosper; it's sure done good fer them.

One day I went searching for one book about prayer in particular. Though it was supposed to be right there on the library shelf, it wasn't. *Huh*, I thought. I went back and checked the catalog system. Yup. It was supposed to be there. "Lord, help me find that book," I said, smiling to myself, and then went back. It still wasn't there. But like Inigo Montoya guided by his sword in the woods, I was not to be denied. I looked behind a neat row of books, and there it was, lying flat on its back, shoved back to a place where no one could read it.

The book was a runaway bestseller from a few years back, *The Prayer of Jabez*. This book was quite the thing back around the turn of the millennium. Here I was, years later, finally getting around to reading it. I guess I'd never realized just how short it was, shorter even than this little book. Ninety pages and change. Very small pages. Very large print.

I started in, and it was . . . well, it was interesting.

The whole book rests on two verses from the book of 1 Chronicles: "Jabez was more honorable than his brothers. His mother had named him Jabez, saying, 'I gave birth to him in pain.' Jabez cried out to the God of Israel, 'Oh, that you would bless me and enlarge my territory! Let your hand be with me, and keep me from harm so that I will be free from pain.' And God granted his request" (1 Chronicles 4:9–10).

In *The Prayer of Jabez*, there is a lot of talk about Jabez and his faith and motivations. This struck me as odd given that the only place in the whole Bible this guy is mentioned is those two verses. And the prayer itself? Just that one verse, squirreled away in one chapter of the book of Chronicles: "Oh, that you would bless me and enlarge my territory and that your hand might be with me and that you would keep me from hurt and harm!" The author of the book decided to pray the prayer of Jabez every day, and he credited it with all sorts of amazing supernatural events in his life.

It's a supersecret prayer, after all—supposedly one that no one else had noticed. Why, you may ask, was it secret? Because it was hidden away in a huge and agonizingly boring list of utterly unpronounceable names. Chapter after chapter of names. Seriously. That hiddenness, I think, was part of the appeal for this author and his audience. Here was a thing of mystery, buried away like a mystic rune you find in a cryptic book.

This is what humans want. We want that one easy trick that will magically solve all our problems. "If you pray it every day, it'll work," the author proclaims with utter and earnest confidence. "Be unafraid to pray selfishly," he also proclaims, which struck me as a little odd. But most of the rest of the book was kindhearted, simple, and earnest, and the prayer itself was easy to remember.

Mostly, that book was about a prayer that gets you what you want. And oh, how we want what we want! How *much* do we want that? For this little secret magic prayer, we *wanted* to the tune of over nine million copies sold, number one on the *New York Times* bestseller list for months and months.

Back then, and even now, it struck me as bizarre that so many Christians would seek out a secret magic prayer, one found in a justifiably obscure corner of the Bible. Why? Because if you follow Jesus of Nazareth, he tells you how to pray.

Not in a secret way, not in a hidden way, but right up there in plain sight, in front of a crowd and where every last person can see it.

***

The prayer that Jesus taught us to pray is there in the heart of the Sermon on the Mount, at the very core of the spiritual and ethical teachings of Jesus of Nazareth:

> This, then, is how you should pray:
> "Our Father in heaven,
> hallowed be your name,
> your kingdom come,

your will be done,
　　on earth as it is in heaven.
Give us today our daily bread.
And forgive us our debts,
　　as we also have forgiven our debtors.
And lead us not into temptation,
　　but deliver us from the evil one." (Matthew 6:9–13)

We also find it in Luke 11. It's a slightly different form there, but the thrust of the prayer is the same:

He said to them, "When you pray, say:
'Father, hallowed be your name,
your kingdom come.
Give us each day our daily bread.
Forgive us our sins,
　　for we also forgive everyone who sins against us.
And lead us not into temptation.'" (Luke 11:2–4)

This prayer could not be more obvious. It is intended to be that way, intended to be both simple and comprehensible. This basic, fundamental prayer that Jesus taught completely encapsulates his life among us and how he asked us to relate to one another.

This prayer is the one I pray every day. It's the prayer I pray on waking and into the inside of my helmet as I ride in traffic. It's there when I'm tired and my mind can't find the words. It's there when I feel so weak and lost I can barely put one foot in front of the other.

It's also a prayer we say, in one of its forms, pretty much every Sunday as part of worship in my church. The liturgist has to figure out how to make the transition. "So we've just been talking about other stuff and praying for our friends and the world, but Jesus taught us this thing we can always say, so let us now say it, saying . . ." And then we all intone it together: a shared incantation.

That this prayer that Jesus taught us to pray is primarily used as a public prayer has always struck me as strange, given that the whole point Jesus is making is that prayer is something best done simply and in private. "When you pray, go into your room, close the door," Jesus says in Matthew 6:6, chiding us for using prayer to make ourselves look good.

The Lord's Prayer is what we call it (or the Our Father, if we're Catholic), and if you're churchy folk, you learn it early and often. It's so well known to us that it becomes like sound itself: vibrations of the air around us.

The Lord's Prayer can become like those prayers I sing every Hanukkah as my little family lights the candles. (Because, while I'm a Christian pastor, my family is Jewish. There's another book there, for another time.)

I know the words—of course I do because you sing them
eight days in a row while trying to keep your kids from setting things other than the candles on fire. Singing in the
midst of fire prevention is a great way to remember prayer.
And so I sing:

> Baruch atah, Adonai Eloheinu, Melech haolam, asher
> kid'shanu b'mitzvotav v'tivanu l'hadlik ner shel
> Chanukah.

> Baruch atah, Adonai Eloheinu, Melech haolam, she-
> ash nisim laavoteinu v'imotenu bayamim hahaeim
> baz'man hazeh.

The words tumble out, familiar from decades of repetition,
woven up with music. But for years, although I sang them,
I didn't always exactly know what I was singing. Learning
Hebrew a little bit helped, as did asking my Jewish family,
which I'd do now and again.

But holding on to the meaning of a thing becomes harder
still when it becomes familiar. Like faith itself, the meaning
of words can be so easily lost.

***

The challenge with this perfect, simple prayer we know as
the Lord's Prayer is that it can become a tumble of vowels

and consonants, a jumbled mass of sounds. We can pray it on autopilot while our mind wanders far afield. Yet the challenge of a thing is often its genius. The very words being so long burned into memory means that the prayer almost prays itself—which means we can pray it anytime, perhaps especially in moments when our own words fail.

So in these next hundred pages or so, we're going to take a walk through this little prayer, sense unit by sense unit, concept by concept. We're going to slow down and pay attention. If you're reading this with others, you'll find discussion questions at the end of the book to stir your thoughts and conversations. If you're reading it on your own, you're more than welcome to check 'em out too. Or not. Whether you do or whether you don't, the goal is to stop and linger for a moment. Deeply consider what Jesus is asking you to pray and how that prayer changes you.

Prayer, if it is to be a real connection with God, must shake us loose from ourselves, drawing us away from the shallow selfishness of our expectations. If it does not, then we don't really put ourselves in a position to receive what Jesus is offering.

So many of us have been well-schooled in praying for the things we want. We've learned to go to God for health, and security, and safety for ourselves and our loved ones—for adding to our property, in the words of Jabez. But in this short, radical prayer, Jesus taught us to pray for what we *don't* always want. For God's will to be done, not ours. To be forgiven as we forgive. For God's kingdom to come. This ancient prayer contains radical potential for us today precisely because its words are *not* our own.

It's a prayer that doesn't promise to give us what we want. It changes the heart of our wanting.

When our desire is broken, what we want so often hurts us. What we want can so often be nothing more than what we have been programmed to want. We want more and more and more because if we are to be good little consumers, we must never stop desiring more. We want because we are afraid of not having enough. We want because we feel compelled to have more than our neighbor, particularly if we don't like our neighbor. We want to be dominant. We want to have power over others.

Our broken wanting breaks the world.

***

Here one might reasonably ask, "But what of our positive desires?" Yearnings for justice and liberation can align with

God's grace, absolutely. The desires for justice and liberation of those who are disenfranchised and oppressed are legitimate, and any resistance to systems of sinful dominance is spiritually valid.

On the other hand, we're still human beings. Falseness and egotism, grasping and gracelessness, the whole gamut of human mess? They're still there, even in the noblest of our strivings. The temptations—for power, for control, for our gain at another's expense—remain. Our prayers are hijacked by those temptations when we take prayer out of the realm of mystery. That drives us to anxiously fill our conversation with our Creator with a river of words, as if this will somehow make us seem more impressive. "Don't babble on," says Jesus. "Don't imagine you're telling God anything God doesn't already know." Instead, he shows us in this most essential prayer how to keep our most sacred yearnings grounded and keep our words plain.

One thing the author of *The Prayer of Jabez* might have gotten right is this: Simple things are magic. The miracle of our existence is magic. The faces of our loved ones and friends are magic. The plain glory of God's presence flaming out into the world is magic. But we can become so used to these quotidian blessings that we forget to slow down and appreciate them, to attend to the reality of what we are saying and doing.

So slow down a little bit with me. Let's take a breath. Then, step by step, word by word, phrase by phrase, let's rediscover the prayer that can change everything.

CHAPTER TWO

How Close the Connection

Our Father

"Our Father" is how the prayer that Jesus taught us begins. It speaks to a very particular form of relationship—a way of interacting that's as unique and intimate as our own relationships with our parents.

While I have known this prayer since childhood, I'll confess that it prays a little differently when you become a dad yourself. One day, being a father is an abstraction: a thing you know must be about to happen because there she is, getting larger month after month in a way that implies something significant is going on. That great rising roundness of her belly moves and shifts and bulges as the thing that is about to happen gets nearer.

And then there's that day when it all goes down, messier and bloodier and harder than you thought possible. The next thing you know, it's the middle of the night, and a tiny little creature is making some pretty impressively large noises that don't take your need for rest into consideration. And you think, *Wait, I'm a father now?*

This seemed, at the moment, pretty weird. I was the same as I'd always been, just as flawed, just as imperfect. Yet here was one tiny human being for whom that word—*father*—was exactly what I was.

There's a strange, passing magic that comes from that relationship, at least for a short while when your kids are small. You're the dad, the daddy, the one who knows everything and can do anything. Got a question? Dad's got the answer (or at least he'll say something that makes it seem like he does). Dad can fix anything (mostly through the miracles of epoxy and duct tape). A father can spin out stories at story time, casting out entire worlds from the books he holds in his hands. A father can pick you up and spin you around like you're nothing, like you're flying, like you're caught up by the wind. It's something I used to do a great deal, swinging giggling little ones around in wild circles.

Now that my boys are taller than I am, it would require the services of an orthopedic specialist if I even attempted it. So it's been a while since that magic has been there. My boys are young men, and I'm proud of who they are, and I've liked knowing them as they've grown.

My sons now look at their father through young-man eyes and can't miss that I am limited and human and fallible. It's a truth I've never hidden but has gotten more obvious to all of us as the years have spun on by.

Human fathers are human beings, the simple source of half of our deoxyribonucleic acid—people like we are. Some of them are wonderful, and some of them are not, and pretty much everything in between. All of them are mortal, creatures of flesh and bone, wonderful and flawed and passing.

Yet Jesus says, when we pray this most fundamental prayer, we are to call God "Father." What are the resonances of *Father*? When we speak that word in prayer, how is that meant to guide our souls?

***

Some challenge the idea of God as a parent as being nothing more than projection: our human longing to recover that fleeting, primal magic of childhood. Sigmund Freud in particular was fond of this idea, which he went on about for quite a while in his treatise *The Future of an Illusion*. God the Father, as Freud would tell you if you were sitting on his couch in Vienna, is just an infantile prototype of your yearning for protection. God is a manifestation of your subconscious. God is an invention of your neurotic desire to be sheltered by the father figure you both fear and require—the one who protects you and your mother, the object of your libido, while also being a threat. You love him, and you want to kill him. Freud was a strange man.

Others, like the more aggressive anti-theists you'll come across on the interwebs, have another way of saying that. "You and your stupid Sky-Daddy-Easter-Bunny God," they'll say, every time I'm fool enough to glance at the comments on ESPN.com. (Why human beings get into religious name-calling in the comments about an article about a basketball game is beyond me.) But the Sky Daddy idea is the same as Freud's, just more clumsily and simply stated. God (or so the argument goes) is a projection of our own desires, which we name "Father" because we're too stupid to see the truth. From that perspective, prayer is nothing more and nothing less than talking to an imaginary friend. Cute when you're five but evidence of some significant neurosis when you're fifty.

Funny thing is, Christian faith has a word for projecting our desires into a delusion we've fashioned to meet our needs.

We call that an idol. And while that's what some suggest we're doing, it's really very different.

Paul lays out his reaction to that challenge clearly in his writings to the church at Corinth. They had a problem with idols, or so they thought. That fractious, bitter church found reasons to argue about just about everything: "So then, about eating food sacrificed to idols: We know that 'An idol is nothing at all in the world' and that 'There is no God but one.' For even if there are so-called gods, whether in heaven or on earth (as indeed there are many 'gods' and many 'lords'), yet for us there is but one God, the Father, from whom all things came and for whom we live; and there is but one Lord, Jesus Christ, through whom all things came and through whom we live" (1 Corinthians 8:4–6).

One of those things was the consumption of meat that had been part of a temple sacrifice, which they argued over angrily. Should you or shouldn't you? But the deeper issue was simple: They made an idol of their own pride. The god of Corinth was, as Freud himself might have said, the ego. The "I."

The way we understand God as Father, Paul explains, is not like that. In making that statement, we are affirming our Creator as both the Source from which we spring and the Purpose that defines us. We are acknowledging that God is close to us, that God is intimately close, as close as family, as close as kin.

In that, Paul is faithfully reiterating what Jesus himself taught.

Jesus did not ask us to call God "Father" because God is a man. The God we call "Father" is not a male *Homo sapiens sapiens* who provided us with our genetic material. *Father*, as Jesus uses the term, does not describe the dynamics or expectations of gender roles in a culture. God is as different from that form of fatherhood as we are from a volvox or a paramecium or whatever strain of COVID-19 is making a mess of our lives this season. God is exponentially different. Infinitely different.

We call God "Father" because faith pushes us beyond our self-absorption and calls us to realize that we did not just magically appear in the world. There is something that precedes us, and on which we depend, and from which we derive our being. We are woven up into that being in a way that goes so deep that we as human beings struggle to evoke it with our language.

But what does that mean?

Jesus touches on that in the teachings that are preserved in the Gospel of John, where that wonderful, poetic, graceful language describes how Jesus felt himself as part of the One he called Father, to the point where it becomes difficult to see where Jesus begins and the Father ends.

"The father is in me, and I am in the Father," he says in John 10:38.

"The Father and I are one," he says in John 10:30.

This relationship goes well beyond our understanding of fatherhood. It's an irreducibly complex interweaving of identity, what one of my seminary professors used to call the Johannine knot, in which Father and Son are both distinct and simultaneously so intricately connected that they cannot be separated from one another. It's a mystic thing—which is not, if we are honest, the relationship that we have with our parents. It is also certainly, from the flip side of the equation, not the relationship we have with our children. Jesus is evoking something more radical, deeper still.

***

In the beginning was the Word, or so John's Gospel begins. Jesus was spoken into the world: God's own Word, God's own self-expression. We are part of that, Jesus says. We are part of that relationship. We are, through the gift of God's own Spirit, knit into the big, comfy sweater of being. Our life, our breath, the atoms that comprise our bodies, the light that fills our eyes, the complex neurochemical dance of our minds and memories, the wild umpteen-billion-year process that gave birth to this moment: all of it is beyond us. We depend on it, completely and at every moment, for the simple miracle of our lives. It is a relationship so much deeper and more powerful than the relationship between a father and child that it bends and strains the meaning of the word itself.

The word bends, but it does not break.

When we pray into that profoundly deep reality, calling out, "Father," we are affirming our participation in all of that. Calling God "our Father" shatters the tendency to make ourselves the center of all things.

We call God "Father" because, from faith, we have come to realize that the purpose of that Ineffable Something isn't random. We realize that woven into our natures is a call to stand in deep connection to one another. Love stands graciously, quietly, yearningly at the boundaries of our lives, asking us to live it out.

CHAPTER THREE

That Place beyond Place

Who art in heaven.

So goes the second bitlet of that prayer Jesus taught us. For a very long time, this was not a particularly easy one for me to wrap my head around.

Even when I was a kid, I struggled with it. "Heaven" is just a tough concept to accept. Sure, there's that mental image of it, with St. Peter and his book at the gate, clouds and harps and everyone you know—wait, check that . . . everyone you *like*—happily sporting a pair of Pegasus wings. That and the dark chocolate fountains and lakes of imperial India pale ale and the shining palaces filled with sleeping golden retriever puppies.

It's a familiar image, but it just never felt right to me. Why? Beyond the sweetness of it, there was this little problem of *where* it was.

The ancients thought they knew, of course. "Where is heaven?" you would ask, and then, like those singing Indians in that scene from *Close Encounters of the Third Kind*, they'd all point up. "Heaven is in the sky," people of old would say, dazzled by the mystery of it. Heaven was behind the firmament: that huge, solid, dark dome of the sky. The Hebrews called that dome the *raqi*, and they knew that in it, holes were punched that allowed the lights that we call stars to shine through. Oh, and there were little tracks on which the planets ran, like toy trains chugging across the sky.

This is not the way we see things now.

We can look across all of time and space, look out past the blue of our sky, past even the dark of our night sky, and into the great deep. And what we see is . . . well, everything there is to see. There is all of space and all of time, falling out and away, deeper and deeper with every passing discovery.

Back in 1915, the big argument in astronomy was about these little swirly smudges that seemed dappled all around the skies. Humans knew how big things were then. We lived, or so we thought, in not just a solar system but a universe that was a huge swirling spiral filled with countless stars. In that universe, there were spiral nebulae, which most scientists back then believed were protostars. Only they weren't. Those spiral nebulae were, as we know now, other galaxies. That discovery meant that the great deep grew even deeper. But in the vastness of it all, where was heaven to be found?

A century after that discovery, we look out with the sophisticated telescopes and intricate sensors we cast into orbit, and we can see light stretching back 13.9 billion years or so, all the way back to when everything Banged Bigly into existence.

When I was a science-loving boy, nine or ten, I remember a friend asking me where I thought God was in all of that and where heaven was, and I struggled to answer. "Maybe it's whatever lies on the other side of the Big Bang," I suggested.

But what if that was nothing? What if it was just this endless cycle of banging out and compressing and banging out again?

While it was infinite, it all seemed simultaneously so painfully finite. It was both vast and defined, both dizzyingly huge and observable, and peering out and back across space and time, it seemed somehow inadequate. Where, in all of this, is the Creator? Where in all of being is this "heaven"—this place in which God resides? Where is that place beyond place?

***

There are books about heaven, of course—the ones that rise out of a genre that's semi-mockingly called "heaven tourism." The stories are usually riffs on similar themes, with tunnels of light during near-death experiences, visits from angels or Jesus himself, the faces of the long lost and beloved. Despite some recantings of such stories, like the sad apology from a young author who admitted he hadn't actually had the experience he described, I don't doubt that most of the people who write those books have experienced something that leads them to write about their encounter.

I don't read those books, though. I'm comfortable not knowing. I don't think we *can* know, not the depth of it. Even if a person has had an experience that dipped them into that chasm, that vastness, I don't think we can know it well enough to meaningfully articulate it. So we have this first fleeting glimpse of eternity as our selves filter it through the lens of the tiny flicker of life we've lived. So what? What does that mean in terms of what is to come? Very little.

And yet, still and all, we hear Jesus, in that one prayer he taught us to pray, placing the God he referred to as "Father" in "heaven." "Care to elucidate, Jesus?" we ask politely. But when Jesus talks about heaven, or about what heaven means, he does it in a peculiar way. Sure, we want specific coordinates, latitudes and longitudes. We want detailed descriptions: maps and schematics and a couple of selfies with Robin Williams and Mother Teresa.

When describing for us the place where God reigns, Jesus doesn't do that. Instead, we get parables—these peculiarly blurry stories, these willful bits of narrative imprecision—one after another.

Jesus describes heaven, yes. But we do not hear "the kingdom of heaven *is*." Instead, we hear "the kingdom of heaven is *like*," as in this story:

> Jesus told them another parable: "The kingdom of heaven is like a man who sowed good seed in his field. But while everyone was sleeping, his enemy came and sowed weeds among the wheat, and went away. When the wheat sprouted and formed heads, then the weeds also appeared.
>
> "The owner's servants came to him and said, 'Sir, didn't you sow good seed in your field? Where then did the weeds come from?'
>
> "'An enemy did this,' he replied.

"The servants asked him, 'Do you want us to go and pull them up?'

"'No,' he answered, 'because while you are pulling the weeds, you may uproot the wheat with them. Let both grow together until the harvest. At that time I will tell the harvesters: First collect the weeds and tie them in bundles to be burned; then gather the wheat and bring it into my barn.'"

He told them another parable: "The kingdom of heaven is like a mustard seed, which a man took and planted in his field. Though it is the smallest of all seeds, yet when it grows, it is the largest of garden plants and becomes a tree, so that the birds come and perch in its branches."

He told them still another parable: "The kingdom of heaven is like yeast that a woman took and mixed into about sixty pounds of flour until it worked all through the dough."

Jesus spoke all these things to the crowd in parables; he did not say anything to them without using a parable. So was fulfilled what was spoken through the prophet:

"I will open my mouth in parables. I will utter things hidden since the creation of the world." (Matthew 13:24–35)

When Jesus opens his mouth, out come metaphor and story. Out comes image after image of growth and harvest, goodness and darkness, value and choice.

The kingdom of heaven is like someone who sowed good seed in a field. It is like a mustard seed. It is like yeast. It is like a treasure hidden in a field. It is like a merchant in search of pearls. It is like a net that was thrown into the sea. And that's just in this one chapter of Matthew.

Every one of those images seems to blur the boundaries between heaven and earth, between "heaven," where God hangs out, and "earth," where the presence of the Creator is a little more difficult to discern.

This teaching about the kingdom of heaven is at the heart of what Jesus told us. It stands at the center of the gospel. But it is also something else. It flies in the face of the way we think about heaven, challenging our tendency to imagine God's realm as impossibly far away and completely different from the world we inhabit.

"Our Father, who isn't anywhere near us," we tend to think as we pray this line. "Our Father, who art not part of this crazy mess down here."

That's understandable, but it's actually a little bit off. Although the fullness of God's reality—the kingdom, heaven itself—may be dizzyingly different from our own, the intent of Christian faith is not to clearly delineate between one realm and the other. It is to affirm the presence of the Divine among us.

The work of faithful people is to assert that there are realities beyond the one we perceive right now, in this particular place and time, and to deepen our sense of connection to those states of being. From that sense of immanence, faith tears down the walls we construct between our lives and God's realm. The work of faith is less about naming the distance between us and heaven and more about noticing the proximity.

***

I pray the Lord's Prayer when I wake. Then, as I walk in the morning darkness, my dog snuffling by my side, I often pray it again, my eyes turned upward.

And on a clear morning, with the moon a sharp crescent, I peer up into the same sky that our ancestors saw as the dazzling heaven. I see it both differently and in the same way as they did.

Differently because I see the morning sky for what it truly is: a sheath of blue-refracting oxygen-nitrogen atmosphere wrapped around a small, rocky world, one that, unlit, grows dark to reveal a near-infinite, star-flecked vastness. Yet the same: a place of wonder, filled with the presence of the One who created it all, and we are both beneath it and part of it.

CHAPTER FOUR

Words We Don't Use, Things We Don't Do

Hallowed be thy name.

There it comes, right there in the third snippet of the prayer: the word *hallowed*, thumping down on us in all its anachronistic glory. *Hallowed* is just not a word we use in our regular speech. And yet here it is, inserting itself into our consciousness, as obscure as some lost nubbin of Victorian-era slang.

Most of us are as likely to use the word *hallowed* as we are to use the words *podsnappery* (which means to pretend to be above it all), *daddles* (which are your hands), *skilamalink* (which means shady), or *gigglemug* (which means an always happy person). Seriously, though. We should all use more Victorian-era slang. It's a fine bit of *nanty narking* (which means fun). Some words just shouldn't fall out of use.

But words do stop being used as we stop doing the things that give those words meaning and relevance. Like, say, the words *araba* and *barouche*, *calash* and *clarence*, *curricle* and *herdic*, *sociable* and *sulky*, *tarantass* and *whiskey*. A hundred years ago, everyone who attended my little rural church would have known that those words all refer to horse-drawn conveyances. We just don't use those words anymore because the way of living they represent is not a way of living we're familiar with. They are words we don't use because we no longer do the things they describe.

In the meantime, *hallowed* falls from our lips, and we sort of know what it means. Sort of. We know it's related to the holy—to the idea we should set something aside as special or unusually important. *Hallowed* may evoke for us the landscape of battlefields, or cemeteries, or some somber place filled with meaning. It has to do with the things and symbols and places we set aside as being fundamentally different, special, important in ways that are hard to articulate.

Hagiastheto to onoma sou is how it rings out in the ancient Greek, in which Matthew's Gospel was written. In the English, this phrase reads, literally, "Let it be holy-ized: the name of you."

That Greek has a single word that means "let it be holy-ized" is one of the reasons Greek is so simultaneously fun and headache inducing.

In any event, what would it look like to "holy-ize" a thing? Can we who live in an economy where everything around us is commodified and objectified even encounter the holy anymore? The holy just isn't something we talk about much, let alone something we do.

***

Let's look back to another Scripture passage about the arrival of the holy in the most unexpected of places:

> Now Moses was tending the flock of Jethro his father-in-law, the priest of Midian, and he led the flock to the far side of the wilderness and came to Horeb, the mountain of God. There the angel of the LORD appeared to him in flames of fire from within a bush. Moses saw that though the bush was on fire it did not burn up. So Moses thought, "I will go over and see this strange sight—why the bush does not burn up."
>
> When the LORD saw that he had gone over to look, God called to him from within the bush, "Moses! Moses!"

And Moses said, "Here I am."

"Do not come any closer," God said. "Take off your sandals, for the place where you are standing is holy ground." Then he said, "I am the God of your father, the God of Abraham, the God of Isaac and the God of Jacob." At this, Moses hid his face, because he was afraid to look at God. (Exodus 3:1–6)

Moses is wandering around, and suddenly here is the burning bush: a plain, ordinary shrubbery entirely alight but not being consumed. It is something both familiar and utterly beyond what is expected. He goes over to check it out, and it speaks, which adds considerably to the bizarreness factor.

Moses is instructed to remove his shoes because he is on holy ground, and he is told that it is God talking. After this passage, he is given instructions—and pretty intimidating ones at that. He is to confront power, the power of Pharaoh. He is to liberate his people. No biggie. Just that.

And so, when presented with this wild command, he asks, "Hey, um, just who exactly are you? What is your name?" Moses is then told just who he is talking to and given the name of God.

The Jews of Jesus's day, and Jewish folks today, approach the name of God with reverence. Various Hebrew words were and are used to describe God. There's *Elohim*, which is the word used for God in this passage. There's *Adonai*, which means "Lord." And there's the name itself—the name spoken to Moses just a few verses later in Exodus 3:14–15.

It's a name written out in four Hebrew letters: a yud, a hey, a vav, and a hey. It looks like this: יהוה. Whenever that term is written in Hebrew, Jews don't say it. They say *Adonai* instead.

(Fun fact: the name *Jehovah* is not really a word. It was entirely made up by European Christians in the late Middle Ages. It comes when you muddle up the consonant sounds of *yud hey vav hey* with the vowel sounds of *Adonai*. There's no evidence ancient Jews used that word. I endeavor not to tell this to Jehovah's Witnesses when they come to the door, although I do keep a PowerPoint deck available in case they get too persistent.)

That name, YHWH, is called the Tetragrammaton because of the four letters. While we can sound them out as *Yahweh*, those sounds don't convey the depth of its meaning. Those sounds also aren't the name that rises from that burning boxwood.

"I AM THAT I AM," Moses hears. But the words can also mean "I Am Who I Am." And they can mean "I Will Be What I Will Be." Finally, Moses is told, simply, to tell the people that "I AM has sent me to you."

Eyeh Asher Eyeh, the name is pronounced, I say, fully aware that invoking that name was considered fraught with mortal peril in ancient Judah and hoping that this building in which I'm writing is well grounded electrically. And there lies the holiness of that name, the sense of holiness that Jesus is evoking in this prayer.

This name for God—I AM THAT I AM—bears the sacredness that arises out of unmediated interaction with existence: existence in its depth and power, the root and ground and foundation of all being. This God is beyond language, beyond our ability to grasp and contain and control.

This fact is more than a little overwhelming. Frightening, even. That is as it should be. The holy isn't easy, and it isn't simple, and it isn't mundane. We who live in this coddled, isolated, commodified era have trouble grasping this. "Hallowing" things just isn't something we do.

***

Holy? What does holy mean in a consumer culture? Honestly, it means very little to us, we who filter out danger at every turn. The holy is dangerous and more than a little frightening. The holy is completely out of the ordinary, set aside as beyond the boundaries of all other things.

Holy? It is a place that is beyond the scope and scale of our everyday, both a time and space set aside. We don't have time for that. We rush about, carefully managing every moment, hurrying through life with our every minute occupied or scheduled, our every instant claimed. Unlike Moses, we're in such a scattered rush that we wouldn't notice if a bush gave off an unusual radiance. We're on our way to the next thing, late and stressed, distracted and overscheduled.

The holy? Ain't nobody got time for that.

Holy? What does holy mean in a culture that sells every last thing, that marketizes and brands? Some say that the American flag is a sacred object in our culture. As a Jesus follower, I take issue with any national emblem being declared holy. But I also simply don't believe it is true because we don't treat the flag as holy. How many times is that flag used to sell you something? "Buy our star-spangled product or service because . . . America!" If the flag is used as a marketing tool, that, my friend, ain't sacred.

I can't stand up on my high horse, either, because the holy things of my faith are no different. I recently read part of a little book entitled *Jesus Calling*. It was another bestseller, natch: a sequence of devotionals supposedly spoken to the author by Jesus himself. What struck me was this: the book lets you know that they've trademarked the phrase "Jesus calling." I'm not sure if that means my little congregation can't sing the old spiritual "Softly and Tenderly, Jesus Is Calling."™ But maybe you should check with legal before you hum that to yourself again.

***

So what do *holy* and *sacred* mean in such a society? Is it possible to holy-ize anything anymore? How can we approach the truly holy when we so easily confuse the carefully choreographed with the sacred, the crass tugging of our heartstrings with the shaking presence of our Maker?

We are used to things standing in between us and everything else. We know that experiences are encountered and filtered through something else. We humans encounter reality through words and symbols, which point to things but are not the things themselves. We use our implements as a surrogate for reality, like the screens that now fill our days with the endless flicker of pixels, standing like a shimmering wall that paradoxically both connects and separates us. What does the holy mean to creatures like us, so used to having the world processed for us by intermediaries?

In the face of that reality, we hear Jesus telling us that whenever we pray in private—whenever we speak our relationship to our Creator into our days—we must remember that none of those ways of being can even begin to express the nature of that space where we encounter God.

For a moment, this prayer would have us set our phones on a countertop and fold closed the clamshell of our laptops. To move away from the crass corporate algorithms and manufactured controversies that clutter our thoughts and turn us from the deep ground and shaking change of the Holy. "Hallowed be thy name," we say, evoking a connection that is both transcendent and powerfully present.

We are asked, as we pray from the privacy of a quiet place in our lives, to slip our feet out of our shoes, to tread with care for a moment. We are called to pause in our lives, so filled with hurry and busyness. We are asked to catch our breath for just a moment, to turn our thoughts to the One Who Is, and to acknowledge that when we invoke that name, we find ourselves on hallowed ground.

CHAPTER FIVE

Will You Will

Thy kingdom come, thy will be done, on earth as it is in heaven.

There is a wild blurring at the heart of all the teachings of Jesus—a tearing down of the walls between heaven and earth. In his own person, Jesus etches the will of God into a reluctant creation.

Up until this point, we've been parsing our way through the Lord's Prayer just a couple of words at a time. Now comes a great rush of words. Here, the prayer moves from holiness to a call for God's will to be done—not just in that ineffable perfection far away but right here and right now.

Woven into those first words was the intimacy of the presence of a loving Father, wildly juxtaposed with the distance of an unknowable heaven and untouchable, unspeakable holiness. Now, there's something new: thy kingdom come, thy will be done.

The concept of the kingdom we've already explored, just a little bit, in chapter 3. So let's take a look at the heart of this snippet: "Thy will be done."

It's a yearning, not just for God acting in some future time—some future moment when the fabric of time and space rips open, and everything changes. It's not "maybe at some point it would be nice for you to get around to it, God." It's not "well, do it, but wait until I've made my way through this fifth of bourbon first and ripped off that nasty email to my ex." It's more immediate, more *right now.*

Significantly, this part of the prayer is about intention—but not ours. It's about desire—but not ours. It's about what God *wants.* It's about the divine awareness to do and act.

What does that mean, for God's will to be done here on earth? What does it mean for God's hand to reach out, touch, and shape creation? Is that not, from faith, what we already believe? Isn't everything already *of* and *from* God?

***

I was contemplating these questions when an image came drifting down into my consciousness. It was an image I'd seen years ago of a deep-space object called God's Hand. The photograph had been taken by what scientists call the Very Large Telescope (seriously), which I suppose it must be to get that shot. Pretty sure my refurbished $170 Android phone can't manage that.

I pored over the image: a color-adjusted bit of interstellar beauty. God's Hand is a vast dust cloud, cupped around stars like a hand ladling water from a stream. It's technically called CG4, but the name God's Hand is just far niftier. It's something called a Bok globule, which sounds faintly like you might find it floating in your order of sweet and sour soup. God's Hand is a huge, cold cloud of particles floating in a region of space about 1,300 light-years from here. It's a cradle for stars, 1.5 light-years high, 9 light-years long. It is impossibly huge, existing on a scale that bends the human imagination.

Sure, there are a variety of reasons it might be there. But despite its being nicknamed God's Hand, it's hard to see divine intention in there anywhere in a way that means something to us. It's a vast splot in space . . . unless you take a very large step back and look at the immensity of creation. Then it seems like nothing more than a tiny little smudge of schmutz, no more important in the scheme of things than a single dust mote resting on the screen of your laptop. It is dirt and dust, as we are dirt and dust.

God's will being done? What does that look like?

Whatever else God's will might be, it is something that's always beyond us. God's will, like the dust cloud we've named God's Hand, is always something so much vaster and deeper than we can grasp.

***

The book of Job contains an old story, a retelling of an ancient tale of a pious man. It may have come to our Bibles from somewhere outside of the margins of Jewish tradition. The name Job, scholars note, is not a Hebrew name, and neither are the names of his three friends.

But this story has cross-cultural legs, perhaps because it can seem on the surface to be simple, easy, and straightforward: Do right, and be steadfast, and you will be rewarded. That's how God works. That's the essence of the divine will.

But as this narrative was brought into the telling of the Jewish people, it got richer and more complex. Into a simple story was inserted a subtler and wiser story, one that was considerably more complex than the story we may have been taught in church as younglings. It's a conversation among

Job, his friends, a young man named Elihu, and finally the Creator of the Universe. The story is told entirely in poetry, written in language that indicates it came from the mind of a sage with a gift for the art of writing. It relates Job's faithful challenge to God in a time of lostness and suffering. And it also relates God's faithful reply.

Job's suffering was nontrivial. As the story tells it, it wasn't just that he needed to "spark his joy" or think about "thriving, not surviving." He was barely surviving. His flocks and his servants had been stolen and slaughtered. A storm had risen and killed all his children. He was physically consumed by disease. Life was horrible. Still, he didn't give up on God.

I have done nothing wrong, Job says. I have served God all my life. If I have held up my end of my commitment to God, why should God not protect me? His friends challenge that assertion, insisting Job *must* have done something to justify what he is experiencing. But Job knows he has not, and he refuses to cede the point. He has stood in covenant, and it is his right, as one in covenant, to lodge his faithful appeal.

Back and forth the conversation goes, until finally God arrives, and Job, having been heard, stands down in the face of what he is encountering.

When you ask God to answer, there is always the danger that you'll get a reply. It begins like this:

Then the Lord spoke to Job out of the storm. He said:
"Who is this that obscures my plans
    with words without knowledge?
Brace yourself like a man;
    I will question you,
    and you shall answer me.
Where were you when I laid the earth's foundation?
    Tell me, if you understand.
Who marked off its dimensions? Surely you know!
    Who stretched a measuring line across it?
On what were its footings set,
    or who laid its cornerstone—
while the morning stars sang together
    and all the angels shouted for joy?" (Job 38:1–7)

That's just the very beginning of a looong answer, one that extends on through the entirety of this chapter and all the next, all of which I would have happily included if my editor wanted me to pad the page count. In yet another chapter after that, Job says, All right, I get it, enough already. But God just shakes God's head and says, No, I'm not done yet.

Here, as relentless as a storm, this book of Wisdom lays out the mystery of the divine purpose, casting out Job's travails against the yawning vastness of creation. Here, now, as the book of Job builds its way into its ferocious conclusion, is an encounter with a God who is always beyond our comprehension. Who are we that we'd presume to know what the exact purpose of the Creator might be? It is more than we could manage, more than our minds and our selves could bear.

And yet here we are, in the Lord's Prayer, asking for just that. We're asking for something we can't totally grasp.

I'll say it again because it bears repeating: in this prayer, we are asking for what we cannot comprehend. When we are overly certain of ourselves, when we conflate our own needs and desires with God's, bad things can happen. When we take the expectations of our culture and assume that its biases and hatreds are God's biases and hatreds, we make a shambles of everything around us. That's painfully, heart-breakingly true in the Middle East, and it's been painfully true in countless other contexts, our own included.

Mystery must be—*has* to be—part of our encounter with God's intent.

***

And yet.

Mystery is not where our connection with God's will concludes.

When we invoke God's will, we make a leap of faith. By choosing this path, the person who has chosen to follow Jesus of Nazareth is assuming they can perceive a glimpse of that kingdom that Jesus proclaimed and lived out. We find our purpose in that: a goal, an end, a will that seeks to be made real.

As we pray the Lord's Prayer, we begin to see that Jesus manifested a kingdom and willed a will whose boundaries are defined by a clear and tangible love. Teaching about the release of captives and the transformation of the human heart, Jesus asserts that somehow, in the vastness and emptiness of creation, compassion and grace and mercy are God's intent for all creatures.

This prayer is the assertion that the will of God is endlessly, powerfully transforming, right here in the humble scale of our lives.

CHAPTER SIX

Necessary Stuff

Give us this day our daily bread.

How do we know what we need? We tend to "need" the stuff that the world tells us we do. When I was a kid, I knew my family needed a television. Without it, we wouldn't be able to watch Adam West *Batman* reruns and TOS *Star Trek* reruns and the *Rockford Files* and football.

A nineteen-inch black-and-white TV was what we needed. Together we watched a screen smaller than some laptops from all the way across the room. ("Which one of those little bunches of specks is our team, Dad?" "The ones with the red jerseys, son." "That's not helping, Dad.")

That lasted for a while until finally we got a color set, and we could see the uniforms. Nineteen inches became twenty-five inches with a remote control. That became thirty-two inches with surround sound, which became fifty-four inches and rear projection.

That fifty-four-incher lasted for years until the wildly complex little array of mirrors at its heart began to come apart. A Super Bowl was coming up, and we couldn't risk having something that didn't work, so a replacement was purchased. Two fingers thin, sixty inches, so high def that you could see every pore and every drop of sweat on the faces of the players.

We needed a new TV! It was necessary! How could you have less than that? It would look so small!

It's essential, or so we tell ourselves. We must have it! Like we must have our smartphones, our laptops, and the internal combustion vehicles that allow us to scurry about in our scurrying lives. Are these "necessary" things? Are they essential? What is truly essential usually bears no resemblance to the carefully manipulated desires that our consumer culture implants in us.

Think about your time, your desires, the things that fill your day. How many of the things you think you need represent what could be meaningfully described as your "daily bread"?

***

Here, we come to a transition in the great prayer that Jesus taught. With these words—"give us this day our daily bread"—the Lord's Prayer goes from invoking our relationship with God to speaking to our own lives. And this request is straightforward, as straightforward as it comes: Give me what I need to live. Give me my daily bread.

Digging a little deeper into what Jesus means by "daily bread" reveals something of a conundrum, however. The word *daily*—or, rather, the Greek term from which Bible translators get that word—is *epiousios*.

There's a problem with that word. *Epiousios* actually has nothing at all to do with the idea of "daily," something that happens during every twenty-four-hour period.

But the biggest problem with *epiousios* is that it occurs only two places in all of the Christian Scriptures written in Greek. It appears in Matthew's Gospel, when Jesus says it as part of this prayer. And it's in Luke's Gospel, in the same prayer. That's it.

In fact, up until *epiousios* was written into the Gospels, there's no trace of the word: in any Greek literature, or letters, or anywhere. There's no evidence of anyone else ever using that word.

So what to make of it? Scholars have had to guess.

It's an educated guess, them being scholars and all, one that rises from the prefix and the root of that word. *Epiousios* we can break into two parts: *epi*, meaning necessary, apt, or appropriate; *ousious*, meaning substance, or the nature of a thing—its "stuffness."

"Give us this day our necessary-stuffly bread" doesn't quite have the same ring to it. But that's what the prayer appears to most directly mean.

What in our lives holds the quality of "necessary stuffness"? What do we really and truly need? I need a warm place on a cold night. But I do not need, not really, the computer on which I wrote this. I do not need a hi-def television, or a television at all, or my PlayStation 5 game console, or the countless things that the ads on Facebook keep trying to convince me to buy. None of them are "necessary stuffly" things. In fact, almost all of what is around me and fills my suburban existence is really not necessary.

And yet those yearnings continue. Endless hungers keep growling in the stomach of my soul. Desire upon desire upon desire, whispered echoes from a thousand carefully calibrated advertisements. When one is fulfilled, another five rise to stir our unslakable synthetic avarice.

We have trouble seeing our actual needs. And from that difficulty seeing what we need, we have difficulty being who we need to be.

***

The Epistle of James has something to say about our daily bread and about what matters if that prayer is to mean anything. This letter is more an essay, or a sequence of essays, that establishes the most essential nature of the Christian ethical life. It has been traditionally attributed to James, the brother of Jesus.

James is one of the most practical, rubber-meets-the-road books in the New Testament. By genre, it's a book of Wisdom, the only one in the New Testament. What that means is simple: Wisdom concerns itself with how we human beings need to act if we're to get along in the world.

Wisdom teachings are found elsewhere in the Bible: in Proverbs, Ecclesiastes, and Job, as well as in a number of the Psalms. Those books teach the basics of how to live and particularly how to live so that you are playing well with others and doing well for yourself. They teach that life is to be enjoyed but that sustained enjoyment is best found in moderation and with the understanding that what we need and what we desire are often very different things. James writes:

> My brothers and sisters, believers in our glorious Lord Jesus Christ must not show favoritism. Suppose a man comes into your meeting wearing a gold ring and fine clothes, and a poor man in filthy old clothes also comes in. If you show special attention to the man wearing fine clothes and say, "Here's a good seat for you," but say to the poor man, "You stand there" or "Sit on the floor by my feet," have you not discriminated among yourselves and become judges with evil thoughts?
>
> Listen, my dear brothers and sisters: Has not God chosen those who are poor in the eyes of the world to be rich in faith and to inherit the kingdom he promised those who love him? But you have dishonored the poor. Is it not the rich who are exploiting you? Are they not the ones who are dragging you into court? Are they not the ones who are blaspheming the noble name of him to whom you belong?
>
> If you really keep the royal law found in Scripture, "Love your neighbor as yourself," you are doing right. But if you show favoritism, you sin and are convicted by the law as lawbreakers. (James 2:1–9)

What does not matter, so far as this little section of James is concerned, is wealth and power. We see shine and sparkle and immediately assume that it confers some superiority to an individual. Those people have nice things, they dress well, they are surrounded by the trappings of material prosperity: that must mean something, right?

Here, living in this culture and this age, we encounter a challenge. We prefer the rich so much so that this becomes our goal for ourselves. The trappings of wealth become our own desire, our own yearning. We have been trained to want the larger and the brighter and the "better." It is this desire—this hunger—that lines us up, our minds filled with fantasy, whenever the Powerball gets to the billion-dollar mark.

The words Jesus offers up in his little prayer directly challenge that yearning. Want only what is truly necessary for your life, Jesus says.

But how do we even know what that *is*? How can we tell, we who live in a society that feels like it is so disconnected from the real that "necessary" seems like a dream?

***

There's a word I've known for years, one that's been surfacing frequently in my reading during the last few years. It's a German word, one that's used in the archaic dialect spoken by the Old Order Amish. One of the core values of the Amish folk, in the peculiar version of German they still speak (known as Pennsylvania Dutch), is *Gelassenheit*. This roughly translates into "calm, contented humility."

It is that spirit of *Gelassenheit* that moves the Amish to set the seemingly strange rules that govern their communities. If a thing makes you proud or makes you stand out from your brothers and sisters? You don't want it because it will tear at the heart of community. No jewelry, no ornamentation, no 5G hot spot in your buggy: none of it.

A phone? That's not necessary in your house, although there's a single landline shared by neighbors. Electricity? Nope, not in the home, although you can have a diesel generator to power your carpentry tools or a washing machine. Tractors? Not in the fields, but you can park one in the barn and use it to bale hay—as long as it has steel wheels so you're not tempted to drive it on the road like a fancy tractor lad.

At every point, *Gelassenheit* is the measure of whether one should have a thing or not. Does an object that you use or have seem simply right in your life? Are you contented with it as it meets your needs so rightly that you don't ever desire anything else to replace it? Does it serve you humbly and functionally, stirring no pride in your heart or envy in the hearts of others?

Or, to put it another way, is it exactly the opposite of Apple's entire business model?

It's a strange thing, *Gelassenheit* is, and the Amish are a peculiar and alien culture. Yet they seem to get the idea of necessary stuffly-ness a little better than the rest of us do. Within their communities, they are deeply inculturated against desiring that which isn't important and finding contentment in the plainly functional and the truly essential. There's no FOMO. No sense of inadequacy. None of the dazzle of carefully constructed influencer product placement.

Gelassenheit restores sanity to our striving.

And so whenever we pray this prayer, it challenges us to remember the simple gifts, humble implements, and places of contentment our Creator offers to us each day. It keeps us connected to what is truly necessary.

We do not always need bigger. We do not always need better. We do not need more and more and more. Our souls—and our world—need us to find peace with less.

CHAPTER SEVEN

The Balance Sheet

Forgive us our debts as we forgive our debtors.

It's hard enough to want only necessary things. Harder still is the portion we'll dive into in this chapter: "forgive us our debts as we forgive our debtors."

This whole debts and debtors issue is a strange thing. The difficulty extends well past figuring out whether it's "debts," as we Presbyterians say it, or "trespasses," as those who aren't as smart as we are put it. (It's *debts*, of course.) *Opheilemata* and *opheiletais* are the words in Matthew and Luke's original Greek—terms that both refer specifically to a financial obligation owed.

This section of the prayer has to do with any way in which we personally are offended by another, or harmed by another, or owed something by another. When someone crosses a boundary they're not supposed to, in an act that might be called trespassing, how good are we at forgiving such people?

Because forgiveness feels . . . hard. Perhaps, we think, if there is an apology or recompense or restitution, then forgiveness will come. We want the balance sheet to line up first.

It's one of those things you work through when your kids are young, particularly when you're meting out scoopfuls of New York Super Fudge Chunk Chip. If the servings of ice cream didn't come out exactly just so, you're going to hear about it. If everyone doesn't get exactly the same amount of time on their screens, you're also going to hear about it.

It's not just, after all.

Those are trivial examples, but the harms we do to one another as human beings cut far deeper. Betrayal. Domination. Dehumanization. Manipulation. The bitter litany of our infractions against one another is radically unjust. Forgiveness is fine in the abstract, we might argue, but only after justice has been done. When we feel victimized, when we feel that another has harmed us or infringed on our rights, we don't even want to talk about that. Given what we've suffered, and how deeply the trauma of our suffering has shaped us, how can anyone expect us to forgive? How can that be a goal?

Yet there it is, set as one of the bedrock expectations of Christian faith, right in the heart of this most essential prayer. What is the place of forgiveness in our unjust, inequitable world?

***

I was reminded of this, often, as I read my way through a peculiar and fascinating book. It's a biography entitled *The Faithful Executioner*, inspired by the real-life journal of a man who'd dedicated his life to being an instrument of justice. Franz Schmidt, who lived in Nuremberg, Germany, in the sixteenth century, was, by profession, a master executioner. It was a trade he'd learned from his father, who'd prepared his son to learn the family business, which was nothing more and nothing less than the art of killing other human beings in the service of the state.

Dad was really, really committed to making his son the best at their trade. How committed? Generally, when we buy our eleven-year-old son a dog, it's not so they can use it to practice chopping off heads with swords.

"Yay, Daddy, a puppy!" "Don't get too attached, son."

The Faithful Executioner is a strange story about a very odd life and about a time that is so different from our own that it's a little hard for us to even process. Here, at the beginning of the modern era, was a culture in which justice was understood to be a carefully structured retributive process. Every punishment was exactly measured out to match the crime, carefully calculated to inflict a certain amount of pain or to induce a certain amount of fear. Steal once and you'd have to pay it back, plus a specific number and level of whippings. Steal again? You'd be hanged from the gallows and your corpse left to rot. Worse crimes? They had worse punishments, which I will not recount because they're creatively, unspeakably horrendous. "Cruel and unusual" really did used to be a thing.

In his journal, Schmidt recalls several examples of prisoners being relieved when they were told they were going to be beheaded. This might not seem like good news to us, but again, having your head chopped off during this era was the "merciful" outcome. It was the sixteenth-century equivalent of getting your sentence reduced to community service—only, you know, with death.

The most peculiar thing about this story was the matter-of-fact way in which Franz went about his trade, convinced he was simply an agent of justice. He was the sword that set things back in balance, or so he assumed, as he meticulously recorded every one of the almost four hundred souls he personally killed, not to mention those he chopped, hacked, maimed, and tortured.

Franz, you see, was a devout Christian and a teetotaler, and he saw this all as completely necessary to set things right and make things just. All in the name of balance. All in the name of setting everything straight.

Which, of course, it didn't. Crime continued, and within a hundred years, the city-state of Nuremberg had collapsed. All that pain, all that death, all that trying to create the balance on the sharp edge of the sword?

Useless. It made nothing better. It healed nothing.

Healing is what Jesus came to do, through his life and his teachings, in a way we clearly haven't quite figured out yet.

***

In Matthew's Gospel, we hear how Jesus wrapped up the Sermon on the Mount, which stands as the highest and most significant of all of Christ's teachings. It's hard stuff. Throughout this heart-of-his-message teaching, he makes a point of consistently challenging the way his listeners thought about the world.

Throughout his teaching, Jesus constantly told all who heard him that our response to the news that God's kingdom was at hand was what mattered. He reminded his disciples and the crowds that gathered to listen that what mattered was a fusion of faith and actions. That means going above and beyond the demands of the law and living a life of radical love—up to and including loving one's enemies. That means being humble and refusing to be hypocritical or judgmental.

Judgmental?

That last part is hard, perhaps the hardest thing of all. When Matthew's Gospel gives us this prayer, Jesus doubles down on the forgiveness part. "Forgive us our debts as we forgive our debtors," he says in the prayer, right there in Matthew 6:12.

And then, in case we missed it, in the verses right after the prayer (Matthew 6:14–15), he says, essentially, "If you forgive others, God will forgive you. If not, you're outta luck, buddy."

Then, in case we've *still* missed it—in case we've space out and managed not to register what he was talking about—we get Jesus right back on us in Matthew 7:

"Do not judge, or you too will be judged. For in the same way you judge others, you will be judged, and with the measure you use, it will be measured to you.

"Why do you look at the speck of sawdust in your brother's eye and pay no attention to the plank in your own eye?

> How can you say to your brother, 'Let me take the speck
> out of your eye,' when all the time there is a plank in your
> own eye? You hypocrite, first take the plank out of your
> own eye, and then you will see clearly to remove the speck
> from your brother's eye." (Matthew 7:1–5)

So it is that three times in two short chapters, Jesus tells us that how we show grace to others is how we should expect grace to be shown to us. He says this once, and then again, and then *again*, because he knows how dismally terrible human beings are at really and truly forgiving.

But perhaps the oddest spin on this whole thing? Jesus asks us to pray for that to be so. Here we are, offering up this pure and simple and straightforward prayer to our Creator, and we *ask* to be forgiven as we forgive.

Does this really register as we pray it?

Here we are, addressing the fount from which all creation flows, the numinous I AM THAT I AM, and we say, "Hey, you know all those angers and resentments that burn like a carefully tended fire in our hearts? You know the way we grumble to ourselves whenever we've been slighted and offended? You know how we take sides, how we attack people who we disagree with socially and personally and politically? That is the standard by which we are hereby officially, through this holy prayer, asking You, the Almighty God, to judge us for all eternity."

This is what Jesus tells us to ask for. Do this to us, God. Yikes.

***

What amazes me, as I pray this portion of the prayer, is that my throat doesn't involuntarily close or my larynx seize up as part of some existential defense mechanism.

Why would we *want* this? Why would we ask God to give us only the measure of forgiveness that we offer to others? Honestly, I think a more likely prayer would be: Please don't do that, God. Judge us by some other standard. Maybe our SAT scores? Yeah, use those. Just not the reality of who we are and how we act in relationship with others.

But Jesus gets us to pray this because this is the way God is. We are judged according to our hearts and according to how our hearts guide us to act toward the rest of God's children. That's a reminder we need. In an era in which corporations and culture support the reign of the self at every turn, it's a reminder we desperately need. Every single time this prayer tumbles from our lips, we are asking God for what we likely do not want—which might end up being exactly what we need.

CHAPTER EIGHT

Your Heart's Desire

Lead us not into temptation.

Temptation is the driving force of our economic system. Temptation is what we live and breathe. Temptation forms and shapes so many of our interactions, so much of what we see, and so much of who we are. Advertising and marketing—fields that aim to get us to want things—is a two-hundred-billion-dollar industry in the United States alone. The ad industry, with its heady blend of sex and power and hunger and fear all mixed together, is a huge part of who we are. We want so much more than our daily bread and the necessary stuff of life.

But temptation? As a thing, it goes deeper than that. Temptation runs in a more subterranean seam than the shallow manipulations of marketing and advertising.

Change isn't easy. The patterns, the routines that we establish through years of writing and rewriting and doing and redoing? They aren't so easily undone. When we try to shift them, to move down a new path, to set old ways aside? Those old ways fight back.

Hunger and fear, sex and power and pleasure? All these things play and shimmer across our consciousness in a hundred different ways.

For the last several years, I've tried to eat healthily. But as I sat in Starbucks while writing this, Lord, was that hard. Everywhere I looked, the world teased me with things that sounded delicious. "Sip a sweet escape," the sign whispered at me, with pictures of some sweet, creamy, caramel, caffeinated concoction. Oh, the delicious alliteration.

I try to write—try to live into my gifts so that I'm being creative or just into that simple satisfaction of getting things done—but there's Facebook, with so many of the people I know sharing their lives and whatever silly thing might have distracted the world today. There's Twitter, or X, or whatever it's being called now, an endless whirlwind of chaos and hullabaloo. I click, and I scroll, and I like, and suddenly an hour has passed, and I've gotten precisely nothing done besides reading a comment thread or watching reels.

I am in Lent now as I write this. I try to stay on the path that I've set for myself this Lenten season—not just of prayer but also of setting aside pointless pleasures, those habits that are simply habits, neither mortal sins nor meaningful. For me, for years, that meant marking the season with an absence of alcohol. For me, alcohol was not an addiction or a pathology with which I struggled consistently. It was just those beers, a couple of them, or a glass or three of wine, or a sip of honey-warm bourbon. A pattern, nothing more. A habit. A simple thing.

But when that was my regular discipline, I would feel the interruption of that pattern for the first few weeks of Lent. I'd feel it like an itch in a phantom limb. I wanted to pop open that IPA as I made dinner. I wanted the taste of a nice cabernet sauvignon, oaky, with tones of elderberry and . . . what is that flavor? A hint of warm outgassing esters from the green vinyl front seats of a brand-new 1972 Dodge Polara.

I'd feel myself wanting the flavor, wanting the easing of the state of mind, even though I'd committed myself to mark that time with that specific change. The hunger is there, that taste in my mouth, whispering to me to be something other than the person I've committed myself to being.

And that, small as it is, represents the essence of temptation. Temptation is that thing that draws us toward what we want the very most in this moment, toward what we want the most right now. It is our heart's desire. It's what we want.

That wanting has nothing to do with who we are trying to become as a person. It does not mirror our aspirations for ourselves. It does not reflect healthy relationships with others.

When we strive toward becoming our best self, we are "integrating" ourselves, which is just a fancy, psychobabbly way of saying we have integrity. We have set that self before us that we strive toward, and we are committed to moving toward it. Temptation? That can test and temper us, sure. But it can also be what *dis*integrates us, breaking us apart, leaving us a writhing, aimless ruin of hunger and anger and soul emptiness.

There is no subtler, more powerful curse to place on an enemy than this: may you get everything your heart desires.

So we ask God, in this most grounding of prayers: Don't lead us there. Don't place temptation before us.

Wait, what? If God is the one we're asking not to connect us with temptation, does that mean God is the one to place it or remove it? It's odd.

But it gets even odder.

***

In the Gospel of Luke, we read a story of how Jesus wanders out into the desert to be tempted. Churches often use this story to begin the season of Lenten self-preparation:

> Jesus, full of the Holy Spirit, left the Jordan and was led by the Spirit into the wilderness, where for forty days he was tempted by the devil. He ate nothing during those days, and at the end of them he was hungry.
>
> The devil said to him, "If you are the Son of God, tell this stone to become bread."
>
> Jesus answered, "It is written: 'Man shall not live on bread alone.'"
>
> The devil led him up to a high place and showed him in an instant all the kingdoms of the world. And he said to him, "I will give you all their authority and splendor; it has been given to me, and I can give it to anyone I want to. If you worship me, it will all be yours."

Jesus answered, "It is written: 'Worship the Lord your God and serve him only.'"

The devil led him to Jerusalem and had him stand on the highest point of the temple. "If you are the Son of God," he said, "throw yourself down from here. For it is written:

"'He will command his angels concerning you
    to guard you carefully;
they will lift you up in their hands,
    so that you will not strike your foot against a stone.'"

Jesus answered, "It is said: 'Do not put the Lord your God to the test.'" When the devil had finished all this tempting, he left him until an opportune time. (Luke 4:1–13)

First, this story is odd because we generally don't think of a desert wasteland as the kind of place that is filled with temptation. For that, we'd typically think of Vegas or some seedy back alley in Bangkok. But the desert? As a place to check yourself for temptation? It seems strange.

And yet it is the desert where Jesus goes. He is called to it. Here, he will test whether he is who he says he is or whether he will fall short. Human beings, after all, do not need outside influences to test them.

Jesus was most surely aware that the test of our commitment lies not in the external pressures and choices that surround us. The most profound test rests in ourselves, in our fundamental identity as persons. If you carry hungers, they'll be with you just as completely in the desert as they are when you are in Coldstone Creamery. If you carry the desire for power, it will ride you just as strongly when you're in solitude as it will when you interact with others. That whispering voice will still tease in your ear, insinuating that you are the exception, that you're the most important thing in creation, that even gravity can't bring you down.

The devil's tools lie within us. Those demons to whom we give authority over our lives are with us always. Those parts of us that we do not want to rule us, that are set against the self that God is calling us to be? They are with us everywhere.

***

Jesus, in that place where everything else was swept aside, was tested because he sought that testing.

But wait. Isn't that a good thing? Seriously, isn't that what we're supposed to do: To seek out those places that test us to be sure we're actually the people we claim to be? Isn't that the whole reason behind the Lenten season: as a time of testing, when we press ourselves to prove our commitment?

Sure. Yet in this prayer, we are acknowledging that those times when we find our faith tested and challenged are brutal. All of us can bear up under it for a while. But to be blunt, we'd rather avoid those times of testing. They are times of tears, times when we feel torn apart, times when it seems we can't go on.

Jesus, as that old spiritual sings it, may have gone to stand his trial, but he was Jesus. And for him, the hardest test came later—not the test that begins the Lenten season but the test that comes at the end of it. When he was in the garden of Gethsemane, alone and realizing what was to come, he was perfectly within his rights to dread it. To ask, as he prayed that night in Gethsemane and as he taught us to pray, that the cup might be taken away from him.

Sometimes, though, we have to go there.

But it is perfectly fine, utterly within our rights, to ask God simply: Insofar as it can be so, can you not test me more than I can bear right now? Can you not lay out my lusts and hatreds and greed before me?

And as we ask God not to set those temptations before us, we are reminded that maybe—just maybe—*we* shouldn't set those temptations before ourselves either.

CHAPTER NINE

The Place of Evil

Deliver us from evil.

What is good? What is evil? Just naming good and evil can be a challenge these days. We are told that such things are culturally mediated, that what is good for one person may be evil for the next. Who is to say what is good and what is bad? Really, what does that even mean?

Back when I was a pup, I thought I knew what evil was. Evil was monsters and the monstrous. I was a voracious reader, the kind of lad who gets sent to the principal's office for reading in class. For a couple of years, round about third grade, every time we'd line up single file and go marching in an increasingly chaotic column to the school library at Timberlane Elementary, I'd wander out with two or three books. Every one of those books would have a title like *Twenty Tales of Terror* or *Seven Spinetingling Stories* or *Five Chilling Reasons Your Child Won't Be Sleeping Tonight*.

As indeed I often did not.

Having read and read and read, I'd lie there drawn up tight under the impenetrable protective force field of my race-car covers and my Snoopy sheets, listening to every last creak and groan of our home, to the faint rushing of pipes, to the wind susurrating through the trees.

Every sound meant The Slime was there, that formless, dark, devouring monster I'd read about in a short story creatively titled "The Slime." It had oozed from the depths of the sea after a nuclear test, as all good monsters from the 1950s and 1960s did, where it had moved through the darkness of night to absorb hobos by campfires and unwitting children. It could be there, bubbling and undulating hungrily in my closet, waiting to engulf and digest me.

Or it could be under my bed, waiting for the deep darkness of night and mindlessly hoping I wouldn't notice how derivative that particular short story was of the Blob. I would lie there and tremble until I trembled off to sleep.

When I was in fourth grade, we moved to England. There, thousands of miles away in a new home, I would recall a Victorian-era story I'd read in one of those books, a tale of bloodcurdling horror, in which one never actually saw the terror but only the poor souls who died from sheer fright.

The story was set in a London suburb and told in a way that seemed to insinuate it could possibly have been true, perhaps, and there I was, with my race-car covers and Snoopy sheets, now living in a London suburb in the very city where that ancient evil manifested itself. I would lie there, fearing evil, wondering how I might ward it away.

That fear of evil, of monstrous things? It's not quite the same in me now. I can watch a horror film and only very infrequently squinch my eyes closed and plug my ears to keep from getting too riled up. Make-believe evil and monsters don't really faze me.

As I moved into adulthood, the existence of *real* evil in the world was what I struggled with: the terrible things and monsters that move about in the light of day in our world. The wars and violence that plague our species. The way we manage to have people starving to death in the midst of abundance. The ease with which we inflict sorrows and horrors on each other.

Evil is something we wrestle with, struggle to come to terms with, something human beings have always wondered about. Why does this exist? Why does God let this happen? And how can we resist it?

***

Let's go to a story of how it all began. Here is an earthy, meaty tale about why things are the way they are:

Now the serpent was more crafty than any of the wild animals the LORD God had made. He said to the woman, "Did God really say, 'You must not eat from any tree in the garden'?"

The woman said to the serpent, "We may eat fruit from the trees in the garden, but God did say, 'You must not eat fruit from the tree that is in the middle of the garden, and you must not touch it, or you will die.'"

"You will not certainly die," the serpent said to the woman. "For God knows that when you eat from it your eyes will be opened, and you will be like God, knowing good and evil."

When the woman saw that the fruit of the tree was good for food and pleasing to the eye, and also desirable for gaining wisdom, she took some and ate it. She also gave some to her husband, who was with her, and he ate it. Then the eyes of both of them were opened, and they realized they were naked; so they sewed fig leaves together and made coverings for themselves.

Then the man and his wife heard the sound of the LORD God as he was walking in the garden in the cool of the day, and they hid from the LORD God among the trees of the garden. But the LORD God called to the man, "Where are you?"

He answered, "I heard you in the garden, and I was afraid because I was naked; so I hid."

And he said, "Who told you that you were naked? Have you eaten from the tree that I commanded you not to eat from?"

The man said, "The woman you put here with me—she gave me some fruit from the tree, and I ate it."

Then the LORD God said to the woman, "What is this you have done?"

The woman said, "The serpent deceived me, and I ate."

(Genesis 3:1–13)

Explaining the existence of evil is the purpose of that story. This is the second of two completely different tales of the act of creation in the book of Genesis. The first is the newer of the two, a back-and-forth song of seven days and creation and goodness, which scholars believe may have been sung or chanted by priests in the ancient temple. That account comes from what's called the Priestly tradition.

But this version of the story is older and earthier, the kind of tale that would be spun out in the flickering light of a campfire, the tents circled for the night. It's the kind of story that would unfurl from the wise one in the group when someone asks, "Why is everything so messed up? Why do bad things happen in the world?"

And so, remembering the story that had been told for generations, the wise one would take a quaff from the passed wineskin, clear their throat, and start in. "On the day that the I AM THAT I AM created the heavens and the earth," they would begin, using that ancient Hebrew name for God.

From that name, scholars can link this to what is called the Yahwist tradition. It's more ancient than the priestly stories, and the relationship it reflects with the God of Israel goes back to a primal, primeval time.

The answer, told in the earthy cadences of an ancient story, revolves around a garden. A man. A woman. A snake. And the fruit of a tree that must never be consumed.

It is there at the center of the perfect garden, and it's the tree of the knowledge of good and evil.

This is not, not, not the tree of knowledge. This is an important thing to grasp. It is the tree of the *knowledge of good and evil*. Up until this point, everything that the man and the woman have known has been good.

By taking that bite, they're not deepening their understanding of what it means to live graciously with one another or in harmony with the garden. They are not growing in their understanding of what their world truly is.

They are tasting what it means to lose sight of their purpose, which is to be helpmates and supports and companions to one another.

That fruit does not open their eyes more deeply to the world. All it teaches them is what it means to be ashamed, to hide from their Creator, and to blame one another.

What is the first thing that the man and the woman do upon having their eyes opened up? They open themselves to social shame, to hiding away the truth of who they are. What they know now is separation and defensiveness, fear and anxiety.

From that place, they choose to pass blame to one another, which can be read in the very next verses. When asked, "Did you eat?" the man does not say, "Yes, I did. I knew better, and I wish I had not." He says, "It was her fault. She made me do it."

When asked, the woman does not say, "Yes, and I am so sorry because this is kind of terrible now." She says, "The snake made me do it." We don't hear what the serpent says, but it might have been, "Everything I said was technically true. Technically. What's wrong with telling the truth?"

So where, in this story, is the evil that Jesus asks us to pray to be delivered from? Where, in the swirl of this broken world, is that evil?

Evil lies not in our mortality, not our small and fragile being. That's just a part of our reality, which can be neither escaped nor denied. Our mortality is our nature, as creatures of earth, as creatures of dust and ashes.

And while we don't particularly want brokenness around us—the sweeping terrors of war and famine and illness that move like a plague of locusts through so much of the world—that is not the evil we should fear most.

We do not pray, "Deliver me from it." We do not pray, "Deliver me from *them*."

We pray, "Deliver me from the shadow of my own soul." That's the evil we need most to be delivered from. Where is evil in the world? It's in us.

My greatest foe is the evil that has laid down roots in my own self, my own body, and my own spirit. I fear the things that tear me from my vocation—those parts of me that turn me away from living out Christ's grace and compassion. I need to be delivered less from monsters than from becoming a monster myself.

When I pray the Lord's Prayer and offer up that call for deliverance, that's where I most focus that prayer. Deliver me, Lord, from the evil within me. Deliver us, Lord, from the shadow of our souls.

CHAPTER TEN

The Power and the Glory

For thine is the kingdom, and the power, and the glory.

As we close in on the end of this greatest prayer that Jesus taught, we come to the familiar, lilting cadence of that perfectly churchy conclusion. The kingdom, the power, the glory: amen!

In the Greek of Matthew's Gospel, the line reads: *hoti sou estin he basilea, kai he dunamis, kai he doxa. Basilea* means "kingdom." *Dunamis*—like *dynamic* or *dynamo*—means "power." And *doxa*—which gives us the prefix for *doxology*, that song we sing after the collection plates go around—means "glory."

Wonderful. Perfect ending to a perfect little prayer. Thanks, Jesus!

Only it isn't actually there in your Bible.

Take a moment and flip back to the first chapter, where I gave you both of the versions we get from the Bible. Or open the Bible itself. Look at the Lord's Prayer in Matthew 6:9–13 and Luke 11:2–4. The line "for thine is the kingdom, and the power, and the glory" is simply not there.

Not in the New International Version. Not in the New Revised Standard Version Updated Edition.

Oh, it *is* there if you're reading from the King James Version and in many others. But it's not part of any recent direct translation. Just isn't in there—because most of the most ancient texts did not have it. A significant majority of the most ancient and reliable manuscripts agree: the prayer does not contain "for thine is the kingdom, and the power, and the glory." Most ancient authorities indicate that the prayer originally in Matthew was almost identical to the prayer we find in Luke 11:2–4—which ends "and lead us not into temptation."

This final section of the prayer comes to us later, hundreds of years after Jesus, as the communities that had gathered to celebrate and follow him added in a conclusion so that the prayer would end, you know, like an actual prayer.

Without this line, the prayer comes to a screeching halt at "but deliver us from evil." And then what?

So what should we do with this bit of the prayer? Reliable scholarship tells us it wasn't part of what Jesus taught or even part of the story the Spirit moved the earliest church to tell. Do we want to keep praying this ending?

***

A clue—a wee little inkling of a clue that might lead to an answer to this question—can be found in a passage from John's Gospel.

John's Gospel, the record of the Beloved Disciple, is a tiny bit hard to figure out. The way that John tells us about Jesus is different from the way that the other three Gospels pitch out that message. The three synoptic Gospels—which means, literally, the three that are "seeing together"—offer up the storytelling of Jesus of Nazareth. In the synoptics—Matthew, Mark, and Luke—Jesus forces us to use our imaginations about the nature of the reign of God. He invites us to ask: what does the world look like when we are all living according to the love of God? Those stories make us use our brains as we try to grasp the message that Jesus came into the world to deliver.

But John doesn't roll like that. Instead, this much more intimate Gospel tends to record challenging conversations, prayers, and peculiarly subtle sayings that play with language in odd, mystical ways. Unlike Mark and Matthew and Luke, John's focus is not God's kingdom here on earth but Jesus talking about how he personally is living that reality out.

This is who I am, Jesus says. *And this is how you can be.*

In the midst of that telling, we get a peculiar little story. We first hear of some Greeks—that is, Greek-speaking citizens of the Roman Empire who were not Jewish—who ask if they can meet with Jesus.

> Now there were some Greeks among those who went up to worship at the festival. They came to Philip, who was from Bethsaida in Galilee, with a request. "Sir," they said, "we would like to see Jesus." Philip went to tell Andrew; Andrew and Philip in turn told Jesus.

The narrative goes wildly amiss from there as Jesus answered them with a strange non sequitur, suddenly talking about his death in oblique and challenging ways. He's talking to a crowd, and the Greek speakers are forgotten, washed away, like a thread of a story that no longer seems relevant to the conclusion. Jesus instead talks about glory and about how the glory of who he is—the *doxa*—is woven up with the glory of the Creator.

Jesus replied, "The hour has come for the Son of Man to be glorified. Very truly I tell you, unless a kernel of wheat falls to the ground and dies, it remains only a single seed. But if it dies, it produces many seeds. Anyone who loves their life will lose it, while anyone who hates their life in this world will keep it for eternal life. Whoever serves me must follow me; and where I am, my servant also will be. My Father will honor the one who serves me.

"Now my soul is troubled, and what shall I say? 'Father, save me from this hour'? No, it was for this very reason I came to this hour. Father, glorify your name!"

Then a voice came from heaven, "I have glorified it, and will glorify it again." The crowd that was there and heard it said it had thundered; others said an angel had spoken to him. (John 12:20–33)

What I am doing, you can do, he says. You are part of this thing, he says. You are called to live this life, too, and to share in it. Follow me and be where I am.

It's an intense teaching, made all the more intense because right as he's wrapping up, he gets an answer from above.

Rrrumble go the heavens, at exactly the moment he's making his point. Some folks hear God speaking. Some hear angels. Most just hear thunder, but it makes everyone shiver just a little bit. My glory is God's glory, says Jesus. And then, You will be honored as I am honored. You will be glorified as I am glorified.

We hear this, and we're like: Yeah. Awesome. Because we like glory. We like power. And we sure do like being in charge of things. I mean, I can't speak for all y'all, but I really like that stuff in ways that are a constant challenge spiritually.

Glory? That's the brightness, the shine, the sparkle, the thing that you look at in wonder and awe. Glory is you lying flat on your back in the grass on a Fourth of July night, when the light and thunder of that fireworks display you're sitting just a tiny bit too close to fill the whole field of your vision, a riot of leaping colors and brightness, the concussive force filling your hearing so intensely you feel them inside of you, deep down. And even though you've seen fireworks many times in your life and you're supposed to be all grown up and jaded, you go, "Wow." You just can't help it. Glory is a whole-body hearing.

We want that to be us. We like it when people see *us* and go, "Wow." We like glory. Glory is what we value, what we celebrate. It is the goal and dream of our culture: to be the celebrity, the influencer, the bright shiny one noted by all, our every post with ten thousand likes and shares and an endless stream of admiring comments.

We like glory, and we also like power. We probably like power even more. We like knowing that we can make things happen, that we can get it all done, that we're completely capable of accomplishing anything we wish to accomplish. We are the master of our to-do list. We will meet every need, will go to every meeting, will do every last thing that is expected of us. Sure, it'll drive us crazy, leave us stressed and in a ruin of mental chaos, but gosh-darn it, we're going to try. We want to feel in control of our lives, our homes, our education, our politics. We. Like. Power.

And the kingdom? That has everything to do with authority over territory, which has to do with power. Here, the place that we rule! This place is ours! Human beings are very, very peculiar when it comes to the places we assume are ours. "This land is your land," we may sing, but we much prefer the line about this land being my land. We'd much rather it be ours.

The early church, the church that gave us this section of the Lord's Prayer? They knew exactly the nature of Christ's power, glory, and kingdom. These three things belonged to God, and they were a part of God. They bore no resemblance to the glory, power, and kingdoms we're used to. In fact, they *subverted* those expectations.

The sense that power or glory is something that is owned and is ours? That doesn't stand because what we're asking to share in is the glory we see in Jesus. And Jesus set aside all that he was for the love of both those who followed him and those who would take his life.

Because it's not our power, glory, or control that rests at the heart of this prayer. It's a power that transcends us, and challenges us, and changes us. That's why we are called to pray "thine" rather than "mine," as we turn our focus away from ourselves and toward God's work in the world.

The early church knew this as the Spirit taught it to them.

This prayer, every time we pray it with our ancestors in the faith, calls us to evoke that glory.

CHAPTER ELEVEN

A Mighty Long Time

Forever.

What do we expect when we say "forever"? Forever, in the event you hadn't noticed, goes on rather longer than we have the ability to wrap our heads around.

It's unsettling, honestly, given the tiny little flicker of our lives, to even begin to try. The scale of forever can be more than a little frightening.

I was reminded of this recently as my evening reading led me into an anthology of H. P. Lovecraft's short stories and novellas. I can't tell you how nice it is to have a break from reading churchy books every once in a while, and you don't get further from churchy books than Lovecraft.

Howard Phillips Lovecraft wrote his peculiar brand of horror fiction in the early twentieth century. Howard was an odd fish, a strange and isolated soul, the sort of writer who lived awkward, poor, and alone. He wrote his stories of alien and ancient horrors in a very particular style, in which every moment is filled with the horror of inhuman madness. His stories teem with monstrous things of mind-shattering scale, who for inconceivably immense eons have woven their eldritch and inscrutably vast machinations around an oblivious, frail, and fleeting humanity.

Musical comedy it was not.

Those writings were profoundly products of their time and of humans' growing realization that everything we knew—our whole history, everything that we are and have been—occupied only the tiniest sliver of a fraction of creation. Before history was a yawning chasm of time—time on a scale that our minds can barely comprehend. As late nineteenth- and early twentieth-century astronomy peered more deeply into the recesses of space, we realized that the universe fell back farther than we had ever imagined possible. Our sense of the hugeness of it all was overwhelming. How do we infinitesimally small humans fit into this?

Lovecraft's writing, clammy and gothic, was the creation of that era, when we suddenly encountered a cosmic reality that was so much more than we had thought. Our first reflex was to block it out, to recoil in terror, the way we might if we glanced over a ledge and realized that it was a ten-kilometer drop. (For Americans reading this, that's a long way.)

The horror literature of this time wasn't horror with vampires and werewolves, even sparkly vampires and hunky werewolves. It was cosmic horror: fear at our encounter with something so different from us that we didn't have any way to process the truth of it.

We don't want forever, not really, because it reminds us of how small we are. We both hate and fear things that make us feel like we're small and fleeting.

Forever does that.

***

When the early church taught us to affirm the forever-ness of God in our praying, I think they grasped the existential terror that it can induce. Prayer, if it is to be a real connection with God, must shake us loose from ourselves, drawing us away from the shallow selfishness of our expectations. If it does not, then we don't really put ourselves in a position to receive what Jesus is offering.

Like, say, in the story we hear every year in church of Jesus arriving in Jerusalem. It's the recounting of Palm Sunday, that annual tale of how a gathered throng filtered the arrival of Jesus through their expectations and came out with a completely skewed grasp of why he was there and what he was there to do. Here Mark, who lies as the storytelling foundation for both Matthew's Gospel and Luke's Gospel, shares a memory of Jesus:

> As they approached Jerusalem and came to Bethphage and Bethany at the Mount of Olives, Jesus sent two of his disciples, saying to them, "Go to the village ahead of you, and just as you enter it, you will find a colt tied there, which no one has ever ridden. Untie it and bring it here. If anyone asks you, 'Why are you doing this?' say, 'The Lord needs it and will send it back here shortly.'"
>
> They went and found a colt outside in the street, tied at a doorway. As they untied it, some people standing there asked, "What are you doing, untying that colt?" They answered as Jesus had told them to, and the people let them go. When they brought the colt to Jesus and threw their cloaks over it, he sat on it. Many people spread their cloaks on the road, while others spread branches they had cut in

the fields. Those who went ahead and those who followed shouted,

"Hosanna!"
"Blessed is he who comes in the name of the Lord!"
"Blessed is the coming kingdom of our father David!"
"Hosanna in the highest heaven!"

Jesus entered Jerusalem and went into the temple courts. He looked around at everything, but since it was already late, he went out to Bethany with the Twelve. (Mark 11:1–11)

If you've ever been to a Palm Sunday service, or if you learned this story as a child, then you probably have a mental image of what you just read. There was Jesus riding into town on a humble donkey, coming through the gates of the city, and it was a great celebration, during which the boys in the crowd immediately started whacking each other with palm fronds they had turned into palm-frond swords.

For most of the crowd, what they were crying out for was the arrival of something they expected. That crowd had a very specific understanding of what it would mean when their anointed one arrived. They knew what it would look like when the great king finally showed up to set everything right.

THE PRAYER OF UNWANTING

For centuries, the people of Judah had been kicked around, battered by one empire after another, and they were looking hungrily for the person who was going to set it all aright. They knew exactly who that would be.

That savior would meet every expectation that had been formed over the course of their thousand-year history. He would be a king in all his kingly glory, just like Solomon or David from eight hundred years before. He would be a mighty warrior on the field of battle, wise and handsome and strong. He would express the will of their God by delivering a divine whuppin' on their enemies, and he would liberate them through the force of the sword or a sustained campaign of angelic carpet bombing.

From hundreds of years of oppression and subjugation, their anger and desire for a big, fierce setting-right burned bright and strong.

That was not what Jesus was bringing. His arrival in Jerusalem and his teachings throughout his brief time among us? They bore no resemblance to that desire.

He knew, as the Judeans in Jerusalem did not, that Jerusalem itself and the power struggles around it meant nothing. Why would he want to overthrow that power? Why would he desire to take it for himself? Soon enough, it would be nothing, shattered and smoldering after Rome had annihilated it.

And then, in just a blink of a cosmic eye after that, the false glory that was Rome would tear itself to pieces.

Every empire in the history of forever tears itself to pieces. That kind of kingdom, power, and glory never, ever lasts.

***

Seen from the forever-perspective of the Creator of the Universe, everything we fight about and every reason we have to wage war and hate each other seem pointless. No, that's not true. It doesn't just seem pointless. It *is* pointless: complete madness, a profligate waste of the blessing of existence, breath, and life.

Jesus saw another path leading us into our eternal purpose. He brought redemption and love and the path of compassion. And in the cheering of that crowd—in their yearning for victory in the immediate now, their desire for power in the context of culture—Jesus would have heard them not getting it.

They didn't get that compassion, radical and fundamental, was at the heart of his message. They didn't understand that the reconciliation and hope that Jesus brought was not just theirs but was also intended to restore all of humanity, including their enemies. It was meant for them but not only for them.

It was a message that was not just relevant in a particular time or in a particular culture. What Jesus brought and what he claimed? It was something cast out of the deeper purpose of humanity, something that runs far beyond our parochial smallness.

The redemption of humankind, through Christ's love, grace, and compassion? That's what we pray for whenever we pray with the early church. We are asking for this great work of reconciliation to be "forever."

Our ancestors in the faith prayed this prayer in Greek. In that language, "forever" is three words: *ais tous aionas.* It means "into the ages," or, more exactly, "into the eons." An eon, in geologic time, ranges from five hundred million to well over a billion years. For those first Greek-speaking Jesus folk, it meant a vast and almost immeasurable amount of time: time on God's scale. And it's eons, *plural*: all of the ages, all times and all spaces, "billions and billions," as Carl Sagan might have put it. It's time beyond count, time beyond measure.

Given the scope of God's work, it's no wonder that people misunderstood Jesus. That's why when those who held power got an inkling of what he was doing, they became frightened and violent. Every time we pray this prayer, like that moment when Jesus came into Jerusalem, is a reminder of the immense scale of things. Against the backdrop of eternity, what matters is our care for one another, our forgiveness of one another, our forbearance and grace toward one another.

That, more than anything, is the joyous, strange magic of this prayer.

CHAPTER TWELVE

Let It Be So

AMEN.

We come to the very last word of the prayer, a word that Jesus probably didn't say when he taught it to disciple and crowd alike. Like the "kingdom and the power and the glory forever," the inclusion of this familiar affirmation was a later addition by the church.

It's a word so common in prayer that we might mistake it for punctuation. AMEN: just an embellishment at the conclusion of a prayer we've mumbled our way through.

This view of the final word of a prayer is a pity, though, because AMEN is a statement of hope and affirmation.

AMEN is one of those words that managed to wander from the Hebrew into other languages—and not just English but every language it encountered. In the Christian Bible, it's one of the few words that goes unchanged when we move from the Torah and the Prophets and the Writings (what you may call the Old Testament) into the Gospels and Epistles (the New Testament). Hebrew has given *amen* to just about every language, and in every language, it means the same thing: "Let it be so."

Aleph Mem Nun, it goes in Hebrew, only backward and with those funny little dots and squiggles under the letters. *Alpha Mu Epsilon Nu*, it goes in the Greek, like some particularly devout sorority.

AMEN is a simple word of deep affirmation, which makes it exactly the word to end a prayer. It is an affirmation of not just what has been heard but what is hoped for: "Let that thing that I have just said be true."

When we pray, there is so much that we yearn to be true. We hope for healing. We cry for deliverance. We long for restoration and reconciliation and repair, of our world, of our nation, of ourselves. We turn our eyes toward a resurrection hope, a hope that our souls might be more tuned to the grace of Jesus and that our desires might be his desires.

***

Like the Lord's Prayer, the story of Jesus's resurrection can become so familiar that we lose sight of it. If we lose sight of it, it ceases to shape us, and the story becomes rote. It is the thing we say because we are saying it, just as we can speak the prayer that Jesus taught without connecting with it at all.

Here, in the resurrection of Christ, something that was completely broken is suddenly and inexplicably *un*broken. A story that had moved in a familiar direction—defeat, despair, and collapse—suddenly moved another way.

Even if it's right there in front of us, we forget to affirm it. How do you say AMEN to something that you don't really let resonate with your soul? How can you say AMEN if the story being told is not somehow your own story?

Early on the first day of the week, while it was still dark, Mary Magdalene went to the tomb and saw that the stone had been removed from the entrance. So she came running to Simon Peter and the other disciple, the one Jesus loved, and said, "They have taken the Lord out of the tomb, and we don't know where they have put him!"

So Peter and the other disciple started for the tomb. Both were running, but the other disciple outran Peter and reached the tomb first. He bent over and looked in at the strips of linen lying there but did not go in. Then

Simon Peter came along behind him and went straight into the tomb. He saw the strips of linen lying there, as well as the cloth that had been wrapped around Jesus's head. The cloth was still lying in its place, separate from the linen. Finally the other disciple, who had reached the tomb first, also went inside. He saw and believed. (They still did not understand from Scripture that Jesus had to rise from the dead.) Then the disciples went back to where they were staying.

Now Mary stood outside the tomb crying. As she wept, she bent over to look into the tomb and saw two angels in white, seated where Jesus's body had been, one at the head and the other at the foot.

They asked her, "Woman, why are you crying?"

"They have taken my Lord away," she said, "and I don't know where they have put him." At this, she turned around and saw Jesus standing there, but she did not realize that it was Jesus.

He asked her, "Woman, why are you crying? Who is it you are looking for?"

Thinking he was the gardener, she said, "Sir, if you have carried him away, tell me where you have put him, and I will get him."

Jesus said to her, "Mary."

She turned toward him and cried out in Aramaic, "Rabboni!" (which means "Teacher").

Jesus said, "Do not hold on to me, for I have not yet ascended to the Father. Go instead to my brothers and tell them, 'I am ascending to my Father and your Father, to my God and your God.'"

Mary Magdalene went to the disciples with the news: "I have seen the Lord!" And she told them that he had said these things to her. (John 20:1–18)

That story begins with the return of Mary Magdalene, one of the women who comprised the inner circle of those who chose to shape their lives around the strange rabbi from Galilee. She travels to the grave and encounters there not a sealed tomb but a stone rolled away, wide open and empty. She comes back running, shouting out that the tomb was empty, not certain what it meant. Two hear her cry and rush back with her to the grave.

Here comes Peter, of course, who in John's Gospel is earnest and well-meaning but a little bit clueless. With him runs "the disciple whom Jesus loved." This is important for John's Gospel because this disciple—one who goes carefully and intentionally unnamed throughout the text—is the one responsible for the whole Gospel. "John" is just a guess made by the early church. Why is this disciple more loved? We don't know. But we do know that on that morning, as this Gospel tells the story, this unnamed person and the Beloved Disciple ran to the tomb. That nameless one found it open, and, unsurprisingly, they didn't barrel right in. They paused, and collected themselves, and while they caught their breath, they watched as Peter just barged right on in.

This is the Peter we get in John, a guy who also randomly throws himself from boats (see elsewhere in the Gospel).

The Beloved remains outside for a moment and then enters.

We hear that "he saw and believed." They're not entirely sure what it is they're experiencing, but they're ready to let it shape how they will come to understand the world. Though the encounter stretches them, they are nonetheless willing to embrace it.

Where there had been death, there was suddenly . . . something else. Where there had been weeping and sorrow, there was . . . something new. That disciple Jesus loved did not yet know exactly what that meant or what that looked like. But they trusted and were willing to offer up an affirmation, a simple amen to the resurrection promise of Easter morning. It's a willingness to stare into the face of a world that seems so often only about brokenness and to affirm that things can be made new, that lives can be remade, that hopes can be rekindled.

That is the purpose of the Easter story every time we tell it.

It is a story that insists, despite the seeming craziness of it, that there is something beyond the darkness of whatever tomb we find ourselves inhabiting.

In defiance of decay and death, our renewal of body and spirit comes from God, who we know through Jesus and his teachings. It comes from God's own Son, living a life filled with God's own Spirit. In the hopeful wonder felt by the Beloved Disciple and in the joy felt by Mary, we have a taste of what truly new life is like.

***

This new life—that transformed, resurrection life—sings in us whenever we pray the Lord's Prayer. Sure, it's short. Sure, we can forget its meaning and let it become merely a rote and empty thing. Sure, it's hidden in plain sight, so masked by familiarity that it may as well be two obscure verses buried away in a forgotten corner of the Bible.

But if we listen to the Lord's Prayer and let those words overflow with their intended meaning, it becomes a prayer rich with the power of God. Not the power of wealth, or the power of social status, or the power of the sword. Not the power of our lusts or the power of our anger or the power of our pride.

In the place of those false powers, we are offered a power that changes who we are. Here is a prayer that does not offer to give us what we want but instead changes the heart of our wanting. The power of this prayer is the power that creates and the power that overcomes.

What we say, each and every time we pray the prayer that Jesus taught us, is not just that we affirm the story that we've heard. We affirm what that story means for all of us as we set ourselves toward the days to come.

We're praying that somehow, in the act of declaring our relationship with our Creator, things will be made anew.

What are we asking to be made new when we say AMEN to the Lord's Prayer? That our relationship with our Creator be as intimate and as personal as with a loving parent. That we be connected with the vastness of being and aware of the sacredness of calling upon that connection. We're calling for an overturning of our understanding of power and setting aside our individual and collective selfishness. We're asking that the distance between our messy lives and our hope for our lives be brought to nothing. We're asking for what we truly need and that our understanding of what is important be made right. We're asking to be held to account for our ungraciousness and injustice and pleading to be turned from the dark paths that seduce us. We're letting go of the desire to rule, to have dominion, and to shine, for all time.

And then we say AMEN—let it be so—to all of that. In doing so, we enable the indwelling of real newness. We are saying AMEN to the change that transforms our memories of the past, helping us heal those places where we just can't imagine change will ever happen.

We say AMEN as we pray that our actions in the present will be altered, our lives shaped to the form of life Jesus lived. It is a prayer that rolls the stone away and sets a bright hope to guide us toward resurrection.

Let that be so, for you and for me, AMEN.

Discussion and Reflection
Questions

CHAPTER 1: WHY WE PRAY—OR DON'T

1. What is your first memory of the act of praying? Where did you pray? How did it feel?
2. Have you ever struggled to pray or struggled with the relevance of prayer? If so, when? What did that feel like?
3. What prayer practices or disciplines do you now have in your life? What part does the Lord's Prayer play in that practice?
4. What does it mean to pray selfishly? How is that different from asking God to change something in your life?

CHAPTER 2: HOW CLOSE THE CONNECTION

1. How does the word "Father" capture your relationship with God?

2. For some, particularly people who have broken, abusive, or dysfunctional relationships with their father, the use of that word in a prayer can be challenging. How do you experience, encounter, or respond to that challenge?

3. For many (like Freud) who reject faith, the idea of God as "Father" is nothing more than projection, a lie we are telling ourselves about the universe. How do you engage with that thought?

4. In John 10:30–38, the relationship between Jesus and his Father in heaven is complex and mysterious, and it could sometimes be difficult knowing where one began and the other left off. How do you interpret those verses? How does that interpretation impact your sense of God as Father?

CHAPTER 3: THAT PLACE BEYOND PLACE

1. When you hear the word *heaven*, what does that mean to you? How do you understand it? Do you believe that we can fully understand it?

2. Is there any difference between God's authority in heaven and God's authority in our lives? What is that difference?

3. When describing God's reign, Jesus used parables, those pointed ethical and spiritual teachings that ask us to understand a thing through narrative. Why did Jesus teach about God's realm in this way?

4. What does our encounter with creation have to teach us about the nature and character of God?

CHAPTER 4: WORDS WE DON'T USE, THINGS WE DON'T DO

1. The name of God that was spoken from the burning bush was unusual. *Eyeh Asher Eyeh* is both holy and polyvalent, which means it does not have a single meaning. It can mean "I AM THAT I AM," "I Am Who I Am," or "I Will Be What I Will Be." Is there one meaning that connects more deeply with you? Why?

2. Consumer culture is alien to the holy. Everything is commodified, copyrightable, and objectified. Nothing is truly sacred. What impact do you think immersion in that culture has on your faith?

3. How do you find holy spaces and times in the rush and busyness of your life? Where do you stop, "remove your shoes," and tread with care?

CHAPTER 5: WILL YOU WILL

1. What is the difference between your will and God's will? How does the mystery and vastness of the divine work relate to your life and what you hope for?

2. We all encounter ill fortune, suffering, and brokenness. How do we understand that in the context of God's will? Does God desire that we suffer?

3. Is there a tension between the compassion, grace, and mercy we encounter in the teachings of Jesus and the often harsh realities of history and creation?

CHAPTER 6: NECESSARY STUFF

1. Do you have all that you actually need in your life? Not *want*, not *desire*, but actually need. What would it look like if you had the "necessary stuffly-ness"? Would you have more, or would you have less?

2. How does consumer culture and the manufactured desire of marketing influence your sense of what is necessary in life? Be honest.

3. In what ways does our immersion in a society that prioritizes consumption prevent us from finding contentment in our "daily bread"?

4. How does valorizing material prosperity shape our faith?

CHAPTER 7: THE BALANCE SHEET

1. What is the difference between justice and grace?
2. Is the gospel first and foremost a tradition of justice or a tradition of grace? Do you think that is a meaningful distinction? Why or why not?
3. In this portion of the prayer, we ask God to treat us as we treat others. Not just our friends but those we loathe. Jesus says it this way: "with the measure you use, it will be measured to you" (Mark 4:24). Honestly assessing your life, do you want that?
4. How do we forgive our enemies? Are there boundaries we set around our forgiveness?

CHAPTER 8: YOUR HEART'S DESIRE

1. Is "may you get all your heart desires" an effective curse? Why or why not?

2. How do you understand temptation? What (and you don't have to say this out loud if you're reading together in a group) has been the most poisonous temptation in your life?

3. Are we at liberty to resist the hungers that subvert our sense of ourselves? How does the concept of temptation relate to addictive behavior?

4. What role does temptation play in the life of faith? How, for instance, is it presented in the life of Jesus? Is there a difference between temptation and times of testing and trial?

CHAPTER 9: THE PLACE OF EVIL

1. How do you, personally, understand the concept of "evil"? What makes an evil action evil or an evil person evil?
2. Why does evil exist in the world if God is the one who created all things?
3. We know that even a good and prayerful life does not mean we will be exempt from suffering or from the impacts of evil. If the cross teaches us anything, it is that. So when we ask to be "delivered from evil," what, then, are we asking for?

CHAPTER 10: THE POWER AND THE GLORY

1. This part of the Lord's Prayer isn't in the prayer that Jesus taught but was added later by the church. Is that a problem? Does that make it less worth praying?

2. How does God's power and glory differ from human social power and celebrity?

3. What would the world look like if we were all living according to the love of God?

CHAPTER 11: A MIGHTY LONG TIME

1. The scale and scope of creation are awesome, terrifying, and humbling. Do you find it wondrous, frightening, or a little bit of both?

2. Given the scale of our lives, how does the knowledge of God's eternity shape our moral choices day by day? If it doesn't, should it? Why or why not?

CHAPTER 12: LET IT BE SO

1. Amen is an affirmation of what we have just spoken or heard. It is also something more, a yearning that we will be made anew. What are the things you fundamentally affirm in your life? What are the things you wish to be made anew?

2. We can only say "amen" to those things that resonate with our souls or that are a part of our own story. How much do you want to be changed by the gospel? Are there ways we resist our own "amen," fighting the hope for transformation that comes when we say "let it be so"?

How and When to Pray
the Lord's Prayer

So. What else do we need to know? How do we maximize the effectiveness of this Prayer of All Prayers? What is the best way to pray it?

Were I another sort of Christian writer, here is where I might give you a surefire, seven-step system for guaranteeing the best possible results from your Prayer of Unwanting Experience©. I'd focus on correct technique, posture, breathing exercises, and intonation. There would be Charts of Unwanting, supplemented by Unwanting Daily Journals lovingly illustrated by Thomas Kinkade. I'd direct you to the App of Unwanting©, yours for the low subscription fee of $1.99 monthly. The first three months would be free, my gift to you as you begin your lifelong journey of unwanting that buck ninety-nine you'll be sending my way.

But I'm not that sort of Christian, and that's not the purpose of this prayer.

The point of the Lord's Prayer is simplicity. While it goes deep, it is intentionally uncomplicated. It is complete in and of itself, perfectly proletarian, open to any and all. You don't need to be a spiritual superhero, a saint, or a Certified Unwanting Coach. Nothing else is required. All you have to do is know how to say it and take it seriously.

Here are a few ideas, which I've tried to make as simple as the prayer itself:

LEARN IT AND SAY IT TO YOURSELF

Knowing the Lord's Prayer isn't hard, even if you're saddled with neurons as flighty and sieve-like as mine. Most of us can manage getting this short prayer memorized in a day, assuming we don't know it already.

You can pray this prayer whenever you feel the need to be grounded, when the world is pressing in hard enough that you need to be reminded of what matters. You can pray it in the morning when you wake. You can pray it as you negotiate traffic or walk to work. You can pray it in your office or on the factory floor or as you figure out what's for dinner.

And you can pray it in the middle of the night, in the liminal space between sleep and wakefulness. Lying awake at 3:00 a.m., fretting about whatever woke you, is the perfect time for prayer—and this prayer in particular.

SAY IT WITH OTHERS

When we incant it together—in worship services, with a small group, at the dinner table—the repetition imprints the words in our minds. We practice.

As Jesus clearly taught, and the early church affirmed, it is the prayer we are meant to hold in the intimacy of our souls. It's meant for anytime and anywhere we need God's presence. For that, we need to remember it's there so that it falls quickly to hand at a moment of need. Saying it with others carves it deeper into us. Because it wasn't meant to be a public prayer, that's the whole point of praying it collectively: to more deeply inscribe it in our minds so that it stays there.

SLOW IT DOWN

Don't race through the prayer. There are times when the stress and press of the day or one cup of coffee too many will scatter our souls. We can realize, while saying it, that we're not really paying attention.

When that happens, stop. Slow down. Say it again. If your fluttering brain is still popcorning and distracted, try yet again and keep trying until you're there with it. Don't force it into your pace. Let it slow you and center you in itself.

SING IT

After several months of praying the Lord's Prayer frequently, I found the rote-ness creeping in. I found myself rushing through it, not really paying attention to what I was saying. The more hurried I was, the less present I was. I needed to force myself to slow down.

So I started to sing it. The tune, a faintly monastic chant, just sort of popped into my head. It wasn't a song I'd heard before but one utterly idiosyncratic to my own peculiar brain. I'd sing it out loud. I'd subvocalize it. But for years, that was how I prayed.

Singing keeps the pace of the prayer slow. It means we linger on each moment of meaning.

Need inspiration? Just listen to others sing it. Google "Lord's Prayer song" or "Lord's Prayer chant" and you'll find a multitude of musical renditions. Listen to Stravinsky's sublime Отче наш, sung in the High Slavonic of the Eastern Orthodox tradition. Or Arvo Pärt's ethereal *Vater Unser.* Or Pastor T. L. Barrett's sweet 1970s Lord's Prayer groove. Whatever stirs your heart to sing.

SAY IT IN ANOTHER TRANSLATION OR PARAPHRASE

Every once in a while, it's worth saying the prayer in a translation of the Bible that you rarely use. You'll probably return to the version you're most familiar with when you're lying in bed in the middle of the night, but if you long for fresh wording for the prayer, encountering it in different translations can be productive.

There are also lots of paraphrases of the Lord's Prayer out there; you can Google them at your leisure. You could, if you so choose, even write your own. God welcomes all our prayers.

With that said, it's worth dropping in a caveat or three.

How does the language used in the paraphrase you're drawn to stay true to the intent of the prayer? Is the path the new wording illuminates the same path, or does it point in a different conceptual direction? If it's the former, then we're praying with a great cloud of spiritual ancestors and saints. If it's the latter, we may be overwriting it with our own interests.

If we're calling it the prayer that Jesus taught—a prayer that marks us as disciples of a teacher—then we should be mindful that we do not colonize it with our own intent. One of the great purposes of this prayer is to free us from the whited sepulcher of our ego, to turn us away from our individual and collective selfishness. If we are rewording it to meet our desires and ideological expectations rather than allowing it to shake and transform those desires, what are we doing? If our interpretation does not continually challenge us and deepen our faith, then perhaps we need to reconsider that interpretation.

SAY IT OR LISTEN TO IT IN ANOTHER LANGUAGE

There's a singular beauty to hearing the prayer in a language we don't understand, one that reflects the peculiar transforming mystery of Christ's intent. Christianity isn't an English-speaking religion, nor is it bound by the language of any single people or ethnicity. It's a polycultural and multi-lingual faith, and it has always been so.

Jesus would likely have prayed in Aramaic, which was translated into common Greek, which was then translated into Latin, where in the Western Church it remained for a good long while. In Latin, the Lord's Prayer reads like this:

Pater Noster, qui es in caelis, sanctificetur nomen tuum. Adveniat regnum tuum. Fiat voluntas tua, sicut in caelo et in terra. Panem nostrum quotidianum da nobis hodie, et dimitte nobis debita nostra sicut et nos dimittimus debitoribus nostris.

It's the same prayer, and as our language was informed by Latin, we can recognize bits of it. But because every language has idiosyncratic constructions in structure and meaning, it's not precisely the same. Or look at the similarities between the Latin and the Spanish versions:

Padre nuestro, que estás en el cielo. Santificado sea tu nombre. Venga tu reino. Hágase tu voluntad en la tierra como en el cielo. Danos hoy nuestro pan de cada día. Perdona nuestras ofensas, como también nosotros perdonamos a los que nos ofenden. No nos dejes caer en tentación y líbranos del mal. Amén.

As a Romance language, Spanish bears a closer resemblance to Latin than modern English. There are considerably more native Spanish-speaking Christians in the world than Christians whose native language is English.

Or what about the following versions in Korean and Amharic, respectively:

하늘에 계신 우리 아버지, 아버지의 이름이 거룩하게 되시며, 아버지의 나라가 오시며, 아버지의 뜻이 하늘에서와 같이 땅에서도 이루어지소서. 오늘 우리에게 일용할 양식을 주시고 우리가 우리에게 있는 죄를 용서하듯 우리도 남을 용서하게 하소서. 우리를 시험에 들게 하지 마소서, 다만 악에서 구하소서. 대개 이는 아버지의 나라와 권세와 영광이 영원히 있사오며, 아멘.

በሰማይ ፡ የምትኖር ፡ አባታችን ፡ ሆይ ፡ ስምህ ፡ ይመስገን ፡ መንግሥትህ ፡ ይምጣ ፈቃድህ ፡ በሰማይ ፡ እንደሆነ ፡ እንዲሁም ፡ በምድር ፡ ይሁን ፡፡ የዕለት ፡ እንጀራችንን ፡ ዛሬ ፡ ስጠን ፡ እኛ ፡ የበደሉንን ፡ ይቅር ፡ እንደምንል ፡ በደላችንን ፡ ይቅር ፡ በልልን ፡ ከክፉ ፡ ሁሉ ፡ ሰውረን ፡ እንጂ ፡ ወደ ፡ ፈተና ፡ አታግባን ፡፡ አሜን

Christian faith is a vital and profound part of both Korean and Ethiopian cultures. In the case of the Ethiopian Orthodox Tewahedo Church, they've been Christian for centuries longer than my Scots-Irish ancestors. But most native English speakers look at the *Hangul* (Korean) and *Fidal* (Amharic) script and are clueless about where to even begin.

These prayers *are* the Lord's Prayer, even though they are utterly different in form, sound, and linguistic structure. They serve the same sacred purpose. If we open ourselves to it, the power of the Lord's Prayer to change us can speak across a hundred tongues. It takes as many forms as can be filled with the Holy Spirit.

Beyond those recommendations, I don't have much else for you. Again, just commit the prayer to mind, take it to heart, and use it as Jesus asked.

The prayer that Jesus taught us to pray really is that simple. It's right there, whenever you need it. It's like air. Like gravity. Like the beating of your heart.

Acknowledgments

To the good folks at Poolesville Presbyterian, my thanks for listening your way through most of these reflections on Sunday mornings. To Kathleen, for your enthusiasm for this little book and the serendipitous cleaning of your office. To Valerie, for again taking my words and making them say what I meant them to say. To Dad, for being my first reader and for the depth of your encouragement. I miss you.

And to you, for reading this. Thanks for taking the time. I hope you find a little grace in it and that it casts a light on your journey.